THOMAS ALGUIRE

How to Train for an Ultramarathon in 2 Weeks

My Crazy Journey in Running

I tried to remember the events to the best of my knowledge, everyone named in the book helped me in a great way and I appreciate everything they have done for me. You have inspired me to do these crazy things and I hope I have inspired you.

First edition

ISBN: 979-8-218-03441-2

Editing by Andrea Gilson

This book was professionally typeset on Reedsy.
Find out more at reedsy.com

Contents

1

Preface

- You can learn a lot about yourself when faced with adversity. The point of this book is to show what you are capable of if you give yourself a chance. I'm not the fastest or the strongest runner but I assure you I will make you believe I am. When I first started running, I had no idea what an ultra marathon was. The term OCR was never mentioned. I would have never dreamed of doing a multi-day event like the *Death Race* or *SISU*. Running opened my eyes, not just to what was out there, but to what I was able to accomplish. These events do not define me but they show who I was meant to be—a person that will always be willing to help, someone who isn't afraid of a challenge, and a mentor to those willing to listen. This book isn't going to give you a training plan, but hopefully will inspire you to get out and try something new. I went out of my comfort zone looking for adventure and to find myself. This is a compilation of my epic adventures and how I became a better person because of them.

2

2015/2016

When I signed up for that first 5k, I had the preconceived notion that I was not a runner. I wasn't in shape; I didn't own any running gear, fancy running shoes, or shorts. I was going to stick out like a sore thumb. I'm not exactly sure what I was feeling at the moment when I signed up, but I can probably guess that it was something to the effect of "who pays to run?"

You always hear stories of how people became runners. There's usually a catalyst that propels the person to start their journey. Mine was just me trying to lose weight. I would go for a two mile run around the house—nothing fast, nothing super slow, and usually I would walk after one mile. I was just trying to move and years of not exercising had caught up to me. I wasn't massively overweight. This isn't a story of how I magically lost a crazy amount of weight and became an inspiration.

It's funny how the story starts with an injury and almost ended with one as well. My life had hit rock bottom, I was the worst off I had been yet. I had just moved out of my home after learning that my wife had been cheating on me. In a fit of rage, I broke my foot jumping down a flight of stairs. It took a few days for me to go to the hospital to get it checked out. They said it was sprained and I would just need to wrap it. This would be why I don't trust doctors. After a few weeks of being in excruciating pain and still walking on it, I finally decided to get a second opinion. My foot was broken in three spots. They were amazed I was able to walk on it. It would take a few months to heal.

I signed up Alexis, my daughter, for Tae Kwon Do. I would also join after being suckered in. This would get me moving and I fell in love with sparring. Sparring would also be my downfall. On the day I went to check out Mixed Martial Art classes, I went to a sparring class. I would tear my calf the day before Thanksgiving. I heard a loud pop and I couldn't put weight on my right leg. I was out for a few months but I would come back and just stick to Tae Kwon Do. I had been going out with Amy for about a year now, and she and her kids joined too.

Amy suggested we do the *Erie County Fair 5k*, we would get tickets to the fair at the very least. I wasn't a runner, yeah I did Tae Kwon Do, but that was for fun. Could I even run three miles without stopping? What if I place last? So many things were going through my head— this isn't for me, I like running by myself, and what's the point of paying when I can just run the same course for free? Fine, at least we get free parking and tickets to the fair. How hard could it be? We showed up after Amy was done with work. We had enough time to get our bibs and our swag bag. Interestingly, you get a shirt and a whole bunch of random things for running a race. We took the stuff to the car and got ready to run.

There were a lot of people, just over 600. This was insane, why were there so many people to run this race? Man, I hoped I wouldn't come in last. I would just run the best I could. This was before I learned to run my own race and try not to compete with everyone. Competition is good but if you're new to a sport, you are entering new territory. This was before I learned to pace myself. Now it seems silly to pace myself for a 5k, but a lesson learned the hard way. I went out way too hard in the first mile and burned myself out. There were so many people out there cheering us on. Even the people passing me would smile, wave, or say hi. This is different. It feels good to have support. I'm not doing great but nobody cares. I'm not last. I finished in twenty-eight minutes.

Boom, my first official 5k and I didn't come in last. I actually did ok. I would go on to do more local 5k's including *Connor's 5k* and the *Texas Roadhouse Running for the Cure.* In the Texas Roadhouse race I would actually get first place in my age group and I won a free dinner entree. Wow, you can actually win stuff running? In the Connor's race, I got second but with my terrible handwriting, they put my name in wrong. I shall forever be known as Thanas Alguire, not Thomas. Such is life, I will write more clearly from now on. I was content running 5ks and signed up for more the next year. Was there more on the horizon?

2016 Spartan Sprint Pittsburgh

Let's sign up for a half marathon. It sounded like a good idea at the time. It was a little after the *Erie County 5k* in August so that would give me two months to train. I decided that the *EVL half* in Ellicottville would be a fun one. Before that, my sister Alicia told me about this race called *Spartan.* It was more than just a run; it had spear throws and obstacles. Luckily enough, there was one in Pittsburgh. It was a little pricey compared to a 5k. I was pretty happy paying $20–$30 for 5ks but $130 for a race was a little crazy. Who would pay that much to run through the mud? There was a similar event in Erie, PA. It was half the price for 10 miles.

What is an obstacle course race? It seems extreme but basically it's running with obstacles laid out on the course. Depending on the course, they could be next to each other or spread out. The *Beast on the Bay* was a 10 mile obstacle course at Presque Isle State Park. The cost was about $80 and it was only an hour and a half drive down. I asked my sister to do it with me and she agreed but then bailed on me. I was going solo. On the ride down I was so nervous, I had no idea what to expect. I was in slightly better shape, but I had never run while enduring obstacles. What if I couldn't do them?

When I arrived, I had to park and then got bussed over to the start line. Where you parked was right at the finish line. This was different, you had to get back to the finish, instead of doing a loop. Focus. I told myself, it's only 10 miles, don't worry that you've never done that distance before. Don't worry about the obstacles, easy peasy. I got in my starting wave and boom, I was off. I still hadn't learned to pace myself so I definitely suffered later in the race. I didn't know this was on the sand. I had never run on sand. This was hard, I was not prepared. The obstacles were actually fairly easy, but I was gassed. I completed all the obstacles but I walked about ¾ of the race. There really wasn't too much running.

Between doing the *Beast on the Bay* and my first *Spartan* race, I would tear my meniscus. It wasn't a major tear but enough that I would have a lot of trouble walking let alone running. Amy had found a discount for the *Spartan* race and signed all of us up. We would do the *Sprint*, a 3–5 mile race with 20 plus obstacles while the kids would do an easier course.

I had a hard time getting from the car to the festival area. This was a lot different than the *Beast on the Bay*, they had a big area set up for vendors, merchandise, and food. There were a lot more people here. This was dumb. I could barely walk. How was I going to do this race? I had a knee brace on but I'm not sure it actually helped. Fine, I'll suck it up and try to do it. The very first lesson I learned was that shoes make the difference. We both had on normal shoes but there was a special kind of shoe designed for the mud and trails.

There were times we were ice skating through the mud, and not gracefully. I still have nightmares of that race. The obstacles were a lot harder. There was a penalty for not completing them—burpees. I didn't know what a burpee was back then. We did not do them. Looking back, I do feel bad but I was not in the best condition to complete them. This also goes back to the notion of running your own race. I won't judge anyone for what they can or cannot do on a course. The goal is to get out there and do the best you can. You will never know if the other person is doing their best or not. Be encouraging and try to help others, this would be the major lesson during this race.

Some of the walls were pretty high and we helped people over them. Yes, even hurt, I still helped out as much as I could. I failed all the upper body strength obstacles. It showed me how out of shape I was. Even doing all of those 5ks, I had no upper body strength. I couldn't run this course. I'll blame the injury, not the fact that I had never run trails or done hills up to this point. This was an eye-opening experience.

I learned about the *Trifecta*, doing the *Sprint*, *Super*, and *Beast Spartan* races all in the same calendar year. I wanted a *Trifecta* but I would have to wait until 2017 to get my first one. It was time to get in shape. I knew what I had to do. By the end of October, I had planned on doing two *Trifectas*.

The EVL half

Now I had some time to recover, but no time to train. You should really train if you are going to do a half marathon, even just a little bit. The only thing I had going for me was the *Beast on the Bay* race which was the farthest I had ever gone for a race. Sometimes you just need to push yourself. This would be that time for me. I look back and realize that I've done way harder things relative to this race but this was probably the hardest race I have completed. This race broke me, not in the beginning but at mile 10, the wall. I learned about the wall the hard way.

Everything was going great. I was keeping a great pace, eating, and drinking. Boom, mile 10. All the wheels fell off. My legs locked up, I couldn't bend my knees. I was literally walking like Frankenstein. I had 3.1 more miles to go. No way, I was done. How could I keep going? I couldn't run, I could barely walk. A woman had started talking to me. I couldn't even focus on what she was saying. The pain was all I could think about. I tried talking back but I'm sure I was just talking gibberish. But talking took my mind off the pain; I just kept thinking, keep moving forward. I started moving faster. It wasn't pretty but it was getting me closer to the finish.

It was downhill from there, no more hills, thank goodness. I could do this. My legs started working again and I could shuffle run. I made it to the finish line. It took me 2 hours and 37 minutes and 31 seconds but I did it. My legs were toast. It took almost a week for me to recover from that race before I could start walking normally. I learned a lot that weekend. Stretching and consuming electrolytes are your best friends to avoid cramping. I wanted to give up so bad, but I kept going. I feel like this was the transition from being content to do what I knew I was capable of to pushing myself. Was I happy just sticking to what I know, or should I push to go further? The sense of accomplishment I felt after these three races would be the stepping stone for 2017. If I pushed my mind and body, how much could I do? I knew what I had to do now—get stronger, and sign up for more races.

3

2017

This would be my year of *Spartan* racing. I did other races but my focus was on my season pass and getting as many *Trifectas* as possible. I would start trail racing, meet other local obstacle course racers, and learn about endurance events. When I started 2017, I had two *Trifectas* picked out. I hadn't bought the season pass yet but we had planned to go to Scotland to do the *Ultra Beast* race. Thanks to Joe B, I had learned about a free training class at a local Cross Fit gym. Prior to this, we had always done our workouts at Chestnut Ridge Park. We would meet at the start of the Eternal Flame trail and head over to the pipeline for hill repeats and once the snow was gone, we would head over to the sledding hill for Obstable Course Racing(or OCR) training.

Joe had his "Pain Train" full of goodies that would help with our unorthodox workouts. There would be rope climbing, rope traverse, log carries, and tire drags. This would give me the idea to build a rig at our house. I would also find giant tractor tires and start using them for workouts. I still have them and they are heavy. My rig is gone but I do plan on building a new one eventually. I had a rope that I hung from a tree and I built my own spear throw. The options for creative training are different when you live out in the country instead of in the city.

A simple run around my block was close to five miles. It was all farmland, wide open to the elements. It would provide great training on days when the weather was treacherous. I learned to run no matter what the weather and started to embrace the bad weather. That provided me with more life lessons and better training than I could ever get from a coach or a gym. People say "embrace the suck." I feel that advice is a lie. It didn't suck, it just was. People had become accustomed to avoiding bad weather, but why? Why is a little rain or snow bad? Being in the cold is invigorating, it makes me feel alive. There were definitely days I probably shouldn't have gone for a run, like in blizzard conditions. Who drives in the middle of nowhere in a blizzard, there are people. I'm a little more cautious about where I run or ruck now.

Joining the local OCR group, I found out about other obstacle course races that weren't *Spartan* or *Tough Mudder*. Those had been the only races I had ever heard of. *Tough Mudder* was known to be more of a group race than an individual one from what I had heard. I didn't have a lot of friends that did this type of stuff. Some people I had talked with about *Tough Mudder* had their grandma go with them. How hard could it be if someone's grandma can do it? That was a terrible judgment call. I learned I should never judge anything on who can do it. But at the time, I wanted to do the hardest races possible. No one I talked to had done multiple *Trifectas*, let alone fly overseas to do an *Ultra Beast*.

Other local OCRs were more family-friendly, especially *Black Swamp Dash*. I would find out about *Shale Hill*, *Bonefrog*, *Savage Race*, *Indian Mud Run*, and the *OCR World Championship*. There's a championship for this? Apparently so and I would go on to compete in it. Each race leads into how my story unfolds. As much as I want to touch on every race I've done, I feel like it would be too repetitive and draw this book out. I tried to focus on the biggest events or most impactful races.

Spartan Charlotte Sprint weekend

My goal was to do double and triple laps in order to prepare for the *New Jersey Beast.* I knew going into it that multiple laps did not count for my *Trifecta.* The point was more for training and getting ready for the *Ultra Beast* in July. I needed to be in much better shape if I was going to do an *Ultra Beast* and survive. Doing multiple laps would help me prepare for the *Beast.* This sounded like a solid plan. The question was whether it would actually work.

This was my first "flat" *Spartan* race. The elevation gains were nothing like *Pittsburgh* or *Greek Peak.* I had a chance to run the race, instead of hike it. I had been running more and I felt more prepared. This was going to be my first "competitive" race. I had signed up for *Open.* I wasn't going to skip burpees anymore. I was pushing myself to be a better athlete. Now was the time to see where I was before the *New Jersey Beast.* I had trail shoes now and running in the mud was so much easier. I was official, at least I felt like I almost fit in.

The *Barbwire Crawl* killed me the first lap. It was so muddy and I did not take off my hydration pack. It kept getting caught and it was completely covered in mud and made drinking it absolutely disgusting. I failed the rope climb and the monkey bars but I had gone farther than I had ever gotten before and was just shy of ringing the bell. Walls were getting easier to get over, I had a technique now.

At this point in the year, I was still having a hard time with upper body obstacles, like the multi-rig, rope climb, and twister. Obstacles like the bucket carry, sandbag, Herc hoist, and atlas carry were getting easier and I wasn't struggling as I did before. Things were looking good.

On my second lap on Saturday, I didn't use my hydration pack and wore only my compression pants— no shirt. That would be the first and last time I ran without a shirt in a *Spartan* race this year. I was sunburned and cut up.

Sunday

I was going to go easy, as I knew what to expect now. I completed two laps yesterday and the plan was to do two more before we headed home. No one tells you that when doing this stuff, you also have to travel home after. I didn't have the luxury of taking Monday off from work. This wasn't making me money and I had to pay for the travel expenses of getting to these races. The season pass only covered the race, not the insurance fee for every lap I did. I learned so many lessons Saturday and did better on my first lap Sunday. Going easy actually made it better since I wasn't overthinking the race. I was able to help out a few people on the second lap with the obstacles. I still wasn't a professional but I did feel more in place on the course now.

Spartan Edinburgh Ultra Beast

Doing a race in another country is a little bit tougher than a local race. Logistics and preparation have to be calculated just right, especially for an endurance event like the *Ultra Beast.* I wasn't as prepared as I could have been for this, but I made due. To save some money for this trip, Amy decided we should fly out of Toronto. We would drive up a few hours before the flight and park. Everything was going great; we got to the airport two hours before the flight left. Plenty of time, so we went to get our boarding passes. I handed my passport over and the woman said she cannot accept my passport because it was damaged.

When I crossed into Canada they didn't say anything but now they told me I needed a new one and I couldn't board the plane. Amy talked to one attendant and got me a flight for the next day. I would just have to go to the embassy and get an emergency passport. She would get on the flight now since it would cost too much to change both of our flights. The problem was that I really didn't have money on me. I had to call my parents and have my sister bring me money so I could get my passport.

I learned a lot about being in another country and how to send an email when you can't use your phone. I couldn't get in touch with the embassy and they wanted me to go to Ottawa. There wasn't enough time. I had to get on this flight or I wasn't going to Scotland. Luckily, I finally got a hold of the Toronto embassy and they got me a new passport. I couldn't bring any electronics into the embassy, like my phone or watch. I had the cashier at the drug store hold onto my watch until I got back. I didn't bring my phone with me. It was in a locker with my luggage at the airport. While I waited for my passport, I went to the history museum. Finally, my passport was done and I had to make my way back to the airport. I got on my flight and was on my way to Glasgow. Amy would meet me there in the rental car. Hopefully, all the craziness was over.

Preparation

I missed bag drop-off on Friday. There was a point in the race where you could have access to supplies. It might have helped a little bit since it provided another spot to drop gear and supplies. Overall, I don't think it affected my race. I didn't really use anything except jerky.

I needed to find another pair of shoes. I love my Innov8s but they are not comfortable for anything past a sprint. I wanted to get a different pair of trail running shoes to change into on the 2nd lap, just in case. We found a shoe store in downtown Edinburgh. There were three girls there who were also doing the *Spartan* race the next day. Little did I know at the time, the one girl was a *Spartan* ambassador named Dashee.

Scotland did not have Gatorade or Powerade, so we got their version of an electrolyte drink. I'm pretty sure I left it in the car so it did not help me during the race. I wish I would have had it since this was the longest race I had ever done.

First Lap

We started with hay bales, a little after we had our first underwater obstacle. When we got to it, there was major bottlenecking. We had to go under planks roughly 3–4 feet in width. They had a safety crew there just in case.

Pacing was going to have to be an average of 25 minute miles to get done by 1pm. Running with Amy wasn't horrible but pacing was slightly slower than I wanted. The obstacles weren't too much different than a regular *Spartan* race, just a little more wobbly. I was worried about some of them falling over as I was going over them.

Stopping was my biggest issue and one thing I knew was that it could cost us precious time. Amy decided around mile 10 that if I was going to make it for a 2nd lap, I had to go on my own. Even going on my own, I just made it out of the drop area by 1:28. This would be my first time completing the rope climb. The best part is that I did it in the rain, which completely shocked me.

2nd Lap

I was dreading going back in the water. I wasn't sure how much more my body could take. Physically, the obstacles weren't the issue. It was my losing body heat. The wind and rain made it even more punishing. Putting my headband over my ears was my only hope of keeping the wind out of them. I was alone for about 70% of the race, the first three miles and then a good chunk in the middle.

I knew it was getting cold and if I stopped, there was a good chance of getting hypothermia. The fog made it hard to see more than 20 feet in front of me. Navigating the course kept getting more difficult. My food supply was not as plentiful as I wanted it to be. I rushed out onto the 2nd lap faster than I wanted to. I forgot gloves and my hands paid for it later. Rain, hail, and snow made this lap harrowing. I had bad thoughts—I knew where the timing mats were and knew there was a chance to cut the course and still finish—I didn't. I knew I couldn't accept the medal if I cheated. I did see a few people cut the course. In the end, they only hurt themselves.

The water stations that were full of bananas on the first lap were empty three miles in. I was on my own for food. I ran into a guy that came out of nowhere, he seemed a little delirious. I offered him the last of my jerky. He definitely needed it more than I did. After he regained his senses, he said we had to go back the way we came. I disagreed and said it was the opposite way. We parted ways and I'm not 100% sure he finished but I did everything I could to help him. The course was a disaster. Later on, the course markings were tattered by the wind.

The volunteers had mostly left due to the cold so it was rare to see anyone at obstacles. By the afternoon, all the metal obstacles like monkey bars were shut down due to safety issues. I reached the rope traverse and finally found people running. They were in rough shape and the volunteer had them checked by medical for signs of hypothermia. I never dreamed that I would be worried about hypothermia in July. It was definitely knocking people out of this race. I was glad I wore long sleeves and compression pants.

Reaching the finish line, I was so happy. I just needed to do the fire jump and I'd be done. Usually, there is a photographer ready to take your picture as you finish the race. Also, there is someone to hand you a medal at the end, but nothing. I saw Amy and that was about it. My joy had turned to dismay. This had been the hardest race I had ever done and nothing. We went over to the first tent we saw and found the photographer and the volunteers. They didn't think anyone was still out there so they were staying in the warm tent.

Fair enough. I asked if I could get a fire jump picture, and they let me redo my finish. I got my buckle and no words could describe how amazing I felt. This had to be one of the craziest races I had ever done. Everything leading up to it made it one of the wildest vacation stories I've had yet.

Of course, you have to sightsee after you do the hardest race ever. We toured downtown Edinburgh and walked way more than I wanted to. It was pretty cool to visit the castle, but we didn't pay to go inside. Instead, we went to the museum because museums are awesome. It was much cheaper too. On our way back to the hotel, we got off at the wrong bus stop and had to walk three miles back to the hotel—active recovery.

Spartan Killington Ultra— **My first DNF**

Nothing ever works out the way you plan it. I had planned on leaving work early on Friday. Amy and I would drive up to Vermont and camp. I had a KOA campsite booked outside of Killington. I was going to run the *Spartan Ultra Beast* and Amy was going to run the *Beast*. I had done Edinburgh and I didn't think anything could be harder than that. Unfortunately, I had to work late and we didn't even leave for Vermont until 6pm. It was a seven hour drive if everything went right, with one stop. That would put us at the campsite around 2am. My race started at 6am.

Change of plans, we got to Rutland around 2:30am and decided we would just sleep in the Jeep in the grocery store parking lot. I woke up around 5am and we had to rush to get to the venue before my start time. There was no time for food, I grabbed whatever I could and threw it into my backpack. I had heard it was colder in the higher elevations so I grabbed a long sleeve shirt to start. I felt horrible with no food or sleep. This entire race was going to be a struggle. I wasn't giving up. I wanted that second endurance *Trifecta*, and to prove that I could do it.

I didn't have time to think once we were at the venue. It was—grab my bib, Amy put my stuff into transition, and I was at the start line ready to go. This was really happening. I was going to do this.

The first lap was rough but I hit transition, refueled, checked my gear, and headed out fairly quickly. I had made it through before cutoff by a half hour. Hitting the other cutoff times was doable if I kept a good pace. I started up the first climb at a steady walk as I was trying to eat while moving. I wasn't hurting too bad at this point and obstacle completion was going well. I had only failed the bridge rope swing and twister.

The first 5–10 miles was okay. I was still moving well. It was after the first major climb that things started falling apart. My up hills were good, but I was going so slowly on the down hills. I couldn't run downhill anymore, my feet and ankles hurt too much. The obstacles that were easy before were now a struggle to complete. My body was shutting down and mentally I was done. I couldn't force myself to move faster, I had checked out of the race.

I just wanted to be done. I couldn't even fathom doing the *Death March* again. Now I was racing the clock to get to the last cutoff mark before time ran out. There were about 10 minutes before I had to be at the monkey bars, which if I pushed, I could have made it. I just didn't have the energy. Every step hurt. I got down the hill and saw they were stopping people from going through. I was done. I was disappointed but relieved at the same time. I had just missed the cutoff by minutes. Time to go sulk.

I went over to the transition to get my gear and hopefully the keys to the truck. My phone and wallet were in the truck, I had forgotten them in the rush. No keys, Amy has them on her. Now

I got to sulk with no food, in the festival area. I think that just irked me more. I couldn't just be alone to wallow. It turned out that Amy was taking her time since she didn't want to wait for me to be done. I can't blame her, since this was my first DNF.

This is why you should have a plan B in case things don't go right. I could blame the factors going in, they definitely didn't help, but the bulk of the problem was my overconfidence that I could just rail this out. There is a reason why this is one of the hardest *Spartan* races. In my first year, I made it 25 miles before missing cutoff. I just had five more to go. This would be my biggest lesson of what not to do before a race. I'd say I don't make mistakes anymore but I do. I just don't make that many going into a race now. Not everything has to go right but when you have that many factors against you, and you mentally check out, it's hard to finish a race. I've improved my mental fortitude since then and learned how to overcome bad things happening.

4

2018

After all of these races, you would think I was in amazing shape. Nope, no matter how much I exercised or ran, I was staying stagnant with my weight. I was hovering around 235 towards the end of 2017 which was way better than the 260 at my heaviest. This wasn't some major transformation but 2018 would be the year I learned about nutrition and how it affected my losing weight and running more efficiently. It turns out that eating a package of cookies on the ride home isn't conducive for losing weight, no matter how much you ran. I started the Ketogenic diet, and I'm not going to advocate for it, but it helped me look at what I was putting into my body. The things I thought were healthy— were not. I gave up chocolate milk for a while, and anyone who knows me, knows that it's my lifeblood.

This would be the year I would start multi-day events, or at least attempt them. I was riding high on all the things I had accomplished in 2017. I felt like I was unstoppable. I would attempt my first 50-miler, sign up for the *Death Race*, and attempt something called the *Cryfecta*. I wasn't done with *Spartan* racing but I felt like I had to branch out and try something new.

Shale Hill

Joe B suckered me into going to Vermont to check out a permanently fixed obstacle course called *Shale Hill*. Even though it was in Vermont, it was not a high elevation course; there were only a few inclines. It was a 10k course, with 70 obstacles. This is where the best people trained. It was named one of the hardest obstacle race courses in the world. Two laps in 8 hours would qualify you for *OCR Worlds*. It was going to be difficult and it was going to be cold.

I learned about a new type of shoe that had metal spikes on the end that would help with running on ice-covered terrain. They were my new favorite shoes. The brand was one of the sponsors of the race. I still have a pair I use to this day. *Ice bugs* help your feet grip on wooden obstacles and in muddy conditions. They are also not allowed on major OCR races like *Spartan* or *OCR Worlds*. The only problem is that they come in sizes 13 or under. I would have to squeeze into a pair if I wore a thick pair of socks or two pairs— which I prefer. It is hard for me to find a good pair of shoes in my size. Rarely can I go to the store and find a pair of shoes that fit me.

We were going to ride up and share a cabin as a big group. One of the things I forgot to ask about was whether or not to bring a blanket and a pillow. There weren't enough beds and I wasn't comfortable sleeping with anyone else. I could have just slept on the floor, but I decided to sleep on the kitchen counter. Life choices—yes it was weird, but it was actually comfortable. It was a pretty big counter. I just had to make sure no one turned on the sink in the middle of the night; otherwise, I was getting my head washed.

Like *Spartan*, there were penalties for failing obstacles. But instead of burpees, you got a chip that you would hand in at the end of your lap. The penalty would be assigned by a roll of a die. Each number was assigned a punishment. Some were silly, most were torture.

The obstacles were hard enough when it wasn't cold but the cold just made everything more difficult. I had to wear two pairs of gloves: one to keep my hands warm and one to make sure my hands didn't freeze on the obstacles. I didn't really have a plan for this race except not to freeze to death. We had trained here earlier just to see the obstacles so I had an idea of what to expect. I had preplanned the obstacles that I might fail before the race had started. I had the goal of finishing two laps. I figured I would have 3 ½ hours for each lap. It's only six miles, I kept telling myself. Some of those obstacles were scary. With the ground being ice underneath, it definitely made me a little more nervous. Some of the obstacles I just touched and grabbed my token, I knew that I wouldn't be able to complete them, and after looking back, I should have tried a little harder on them. I had only racked up about five or six tokens total, which I didn't think was bad.

The penalties I had to do: ride a kid's bike down the embankment and back up, sledgehammer a tire 100 times, battle rope 50 times and over-under a barb wire fence. I had gotten multiples of the bike ride and sledgehammer, so I can't really remember what the other punishments were. I was done after one lap. My problem was that I went inside to warm up and change my clothes. Once I sat down and food was an option, my ambition to go back out was nil. I was happy with one lap. I don't know how I would have done going back out.

Unfortunately, *Shale Hill* is no more. I got to volunteer one last time before they closed the course down. I had planned on doing the *Shale Hell* 24 hour race later in the year but it was canceled. If you had the chance to run any one of the races put on here, you know how special it was. If you didn't get the chance to, you missed out on an amazing course. Luckily there is the *Sunny Hill Viking Obstacle* course race in Greenville, NY near Albany. It is a great course that shares some of the same obstacles as *Shale Hill*.

Beast of Burden 50 miler

What was I thinking? I had just signed up for a 50 mile road/trail race along the Erie Canal. *The Beast of Burden* is the only local ultra marathon in my area. It was just 45 minutes away, so I couldn't say no. I had two weeks after *Shale Hill* to recover. It would be another cold race. I had to be prepared for staying in the cold for 12–20 hours, depending on how long it took me to finish. The plan was to drive up before the race started, which was nice because it started at 10am. I didn't question it because it let me sleep in.

Ian was going to be there volunteering so I had a familiar face to see out on the course. One thing I learned about this race, and it would be important for this race and the 100 mile winter and summer versions, is that it's a 12.5 mile loop. The race starts in Lockport, NY –the first aid station is in Gasport, NY– and the turnaround is in Middleport.

You had to check-in at each aid station. The start/finish line was on the opposite side of the towpath, the side you would be running for the bulk of the event. It's pretty evil that you can see the finish line for two miles but you know you are still far away from it. The first mile is towards the city of Lockport. You have to reach the bridge to cross the canal and then head towards Middleport. It's about seven miles to the first aid station in Gasport. You then head out to Middleport and check-in at the lodge. This is probably the most boring ultra race I have ever seen.

There isn't anything to look at while you are running; there is just the canal and farmland. Every so often you find a bridge. There are landmarks but they are few and far between. The pirate ship, the golf course, the Gasport Marina, and the Elks Lodge are a few that stuck out for me. Running one lap for a 25 mile loop isn't too bad. Running it twice gets really boring. There are too many open fields and then if the wind picks up, you better hope you have something to protect you. The other problem is the sun beats down on you in the summertime. I would learn that later on. The 50 mile course would have 24 hours to finish, which is very generous for a time cutoff.

I was dressed for the cold. I had my hydration bladder in my backpack. I should have insolated it because it kept freezing on me. I learned the hard way that even when it's not straight water, liquids will freeze in a cold race. I had to blow out the line every time I took a drink. I had compression pants on, with my running shorts over them. I also had on my *Underarmour* Cold gear long sleeve shirt and my *Spartan* volunteer sweater. I had these running gloves that kept your hands warm and allowed you to use the touch screen on the phone.

I want to say I prepared for this race and maybe I did to an extent. I felt great getting to Gasport, and after checking in, looking at what goodies they had. All the bad stuff; there was every treat you could think of. Except for *Sour Patch Kids*, which I can forgive because they had things I wouldn't have even thought about bringing. I was in food heaven. I grabbed a few *Hammer Gel* packs and headed out.

Middleport was going to be a better aid station, and it was inside. The hardest part about this race, I feel, is getting out of the aid stations. There is heat and food, so it's easy to get sucked in for longer than you want to. I wasn't super cold but I needed to get off of my feet, and stretch. That was my biggest problem. I hadn't planned on being on my feet that long and I learned that a good pair of shoes can go a long way. I headed out after about 15 minutes.

My last lap I was hurting. I slowed down considerably after reaching the Middleport aid station. Was I going to finish? I couldn't even run anymore. My pace was just a slow walk. Everything hurt. I just wanted off my feet. On my way back, Amy met me at the Gasport aid station since she was volunteering there until I showed up. She was going to walk back with me and pace me for the last seven miles, it felt like 70. I wanted to stop at every point I could.

Oh look, I can sit on the bridge, and there's a park bench. The ground looks nice too. I just wanted to be done moving, I had plenty of time to take a nap and still finish within the 24 hour limit. Amy pushed me. She kept telling me to just keep moving forward. It was the slowest I had ever gone. Once I saw the finish line across the Canal, my mood improved greatly. I was energized, the end was in sight. I started shuffle running and made it across the bridge. Just one more mile to go and I'm done with this nightmare. I am never doing this again, I thought to myself.

I sprinted towards the finish line and I was so glad to be done.

This has got to be the best medal ever, as this was the hardest event I had done to this point. They gave the medal. It was about the size of a half dollar. Where's the rest of it? This has got to be a joke. Well, at least it will fit on my keychain. The sweater I got was pretty nice but they ran out of bumper stickers.

Becoming a Pacer (Buffalo Marathon + Rochester Half)

How could I possibly be a pacer for a marathon? I had no idea what was involved. Technically, up to this point, I had never run a marathon. Of course, I've done crazier things but running a marathon is still a daunting task. People would be relying on me to finish at the desired pace. When I first started running, I couldn't keep a steady pace to save my life. I was all over. There were still points where I would walk.

I had zero experience when I applied, but why not? They'll just say I'm not experienced enough or something. I was shocked when they said I would be a pacer. Now I'd better figure out what's involved. Luckily, I would only be running half of the *Buffalo Marathon* and the *Rochester Half*. I would be pacing 5:20 full and 2:40 half. But since I was doing the second half there would only be marathon runners counting on me. I would be at the halfway point and the half marathon pacer would switch with me before heading into the finish line. I would go on to complete the rest of the marathon at that pace. I've done halves where they had pacers and they weren't super human, just friendly runners who motivated people while they ran. I could do this. Nothing was going to stop me.

A lot of my friends were running the half, and none of my friends running the marathon were planning on going at my pace. The second half pacers were all gathered around the 12 mile mark, half marathoners would split off and finish while the marathoners would continue. I had my pacing stick. No one tells you that it's a pain carrying that stick while you're running, especially for 14 miles.

I swear, if they ever let me pace again, I'm going to figure out a plan to not carry that stick. My pace was going to be a little over a 12 minute mile, which luckily for me, people at that pace don't care as much as faster times. Not to discredit anyone because running a marathon is an incredible feat and these are my people. They're not trying to win. Each person has their own story about why they are out there and it's awesome to hear their stories. Unfortunately, nowadays most runners wear headphones so it's a little more difficult to talk to anyone. Sometimes I feel like you're missing out on so much when you're distracted by your phone, but maybe that's what they need to finish. I can't say I haven't been there, especially going back and looking retrospectively on my 100 milers. You do what you need to do to get to the finish line.

I was standing in the transition area, waiting for my first half pacers to come through. I was getting nervous. It's one thing to run a half marathon on your own, but now I had people relying on me to keep them on pace. Would I stop at the aid stations, or just keep going? I had my hydration vest on, so I really didn't need to stop. The plan is to just keep going. No stopping. I had so many questions that I forgot to ask about this. The pacer was coming and now it's my time to run. Don't panic. You've done way harder events than this.

I had practiced running this pace before but it was way slower than I normally go. I had only done a few miles, not the 14 miles I was going to do today. This was harder on my body since I was changing how my feet were hitting the ground. I shortened my stride to slow myself down. My legs were aching. I was only a few miles in and the heat was starting to get to me. This wasn't going to be as easy as I had thought.

I didn't have anyone around me and I was a little concerned. Was I running the right pace? I was hitting the mile markers at the right time, but what about in-between? I should have practiced more. It felt like I was being consistent but nobody was around. I was running up Linwood Avenue and heard a loud explosion in front of me. It definitely shook me. It was an accident between two police motorcycles. Luckily, no one was seriously hurt. Runners were allowed through the intersection and I just kept going.

People were lined up on some of the roads cheering people on. It was helping me keep my mind off the pain and the heat. Some had sprinklers set up and it was fun to run through them. I heard a few runners complain about the hills which I thought was funny since this was probably the flattest course I had run in a long time.

The tricky part about the finish is that you have to run through the roundabout and then back up Franklin Street to the finish line. This would be my first finish as a pacer. There was a prize for the pacer that finished closest to their time. I was just happy that I wasn't too far over. That was my one problem, do I finish at gun time or the time the other pacer made it to me? That would be a big difference in times. No one complained so I let it go. Maybe next time I'll ask about that.

Peak Death Race

There were rumors that they were bringing back the *Death Race*. What is the *Death Race* you ask? It's supposed to be the ultimate challenge, both physically and mentally. It's not simply a race but more of an experience. You don't know when it starts or when it ends. No *Death Race* is ever the same, and it can last up to 70 hours. *The Death Race* is designed to find your weaknesses and exploit them. The goal is to make you quit.

There was a lottery to participate since it was the inaugural year of the new *Peak Death Race.* Why not enter? I had only done a 12 hour *Hurricane Heat* up to that point and the *Spartan Ultra.* What were the chances of actually getting in? Getting the positive email was definitely a surprise. I'm in, I'd better start preparing.

The gear list changed a few times before the race started. I learned that it can change up to a few days before the race begins. I was fortunate to have a friend who let me stay in her hotel room the night before. It also helped to have someone familiar, to go through the gear list and calm my nerves. Some of the people at the hotel were previous *Death Race* participants, so we got some advice. Nothing could prepare me for what was about to happen. To say the *Death Race* changes you is an understatement. It is a rebirth of your mind, body, and soul.

Gear List:

I'll try to break down everything that I brought and comment on how it helped or hurt. We had to list our mandatory gear and our non-mandatory gear. The lists were laminated and available for inspection.

Mandatory gear:

· The axe—I made a last minute decision to switch to a smaller axe. I've been training with a heavier one. The axe broke three swings in. I had to carry a broken axe for the remainder of the race.

· Pruning shears—I went with smaller shears. For the purpose of the race, they worked very well.

• Work gloves—I bought a $10 pair from Walmart. They worked for what I needed them for.

• Headlamp—I've been sticking with my *Energizer* one. It worked great.

• Sandbag—I needed a 55lb sandbag. I bought a *FitShit* one and loaded it to 58lbs. I didn't want to be under. The handles made it nice to attach to my ruck with carabineers.

• Size 18 *Adams Dry Fly*—I didn't last long enough to use it

• 4—3x5 cards that were inscribed with the words "Apparently I wasn't ready"—I didn't use them, which was a good thing.

• $5 bill note—It was donated to a local girl who was in an accident.

• $100— I'm not sure what they did with it.

• 148 pennies—We handed them in. I don't know what they were for (the rumor was for the laps we did during barb wire crawl.)

• Safety goggles—I bought a $2 pair from Walmart, didn't use them.

Non-mandatory gear:

• Ruck—I went with my *GO-Ruck Bag, the Rucker.* It was a little small. I should have gone with a bigger one.

• Hydration bag—I didn't have enough room so I bought a small bag to attach to my ruck to hold my hydration bladders.

• Clothes on my body—I listed this, as I wasn't sure how specific we had to be. Shoes—I went with the *Altra Lone Peak 3.5* (they were amazing). Socks—I started with *MUDGEAR* and *Balega*. Afterward we had to go shoeless. I just had on the *Balega* knee compression sleeves. They helped a lot, but not enough. Shorts—I went with my traditional *Clinch Gear* shorts. I knew Wednesday night was going to be the coldest so I had an

Underarmor shirt with my *Bonefrog* short sleeve shirt on over it. Hat—I had my *Pokemon Professor Hat Black Swamp Dash* obstacle completion headband—I thought I would represent that awesome race.

• First aid supplies—I went with electrical tape, Neosporin packets, gauze, and super glue.

• Multi-tool—I had it just in case. I probably should invest in a better one if I keep doing these.

• Bungee cords—They made it easier to hold the bucket to the ruck.

• Duct tape—I didn't use it, but it might have helped to tape my knees.

• Sharpie—Just in case I had to write anything down.

• Extra clothes—Vacuum sealed, so they didn't get wet.

• Zip ties—While training, I used them to keep things attached a little better. I didn't have time to use them during the event.

• Trekking poles—Absolutely came in handy for going up and down the mountains, this saved my legs.

•Food—I had custom protein bars made by Amy. They were low-carb, jerky, almonds, and fat bombs.

• Wipes—If you have 'to go' in the woods.

• Extra shoes—I regretted bringing them, the *Altra Lone Peak 3.5* were great. My goal was to pack light. When I saw what everyone else had, I started getting nervous that I was unprepared. Twenty hours in, I realized less weight was a great thing. If I had the sand bag a little lighter, I would have lasted longer.

The Race

When we got there at 10am, we had to sign up and hand in our $5 bill, the $100, and the 148 pennies. After we checked in with medical, we had to go out and start chopping wood. After my third swing, the axe broke. We had to load up the trailers, so I had to jump on that task. After we got both trailers loaded and some wood stacked along the fence, it was time for our first test. We had to hold our axes in front of us until 10 people gave up. Having the lighter axe definitely helped, being broken—helped more. I just held the two parts together. I lasted until the end and didn't get a card.

We were in Chittenden and had to hike to Pittsfield, which they told us was about 14 miles away. Easy enough—well, they had to make it a little more difficult. We had 14 hours to bring a generator and a countdown clock with us. After about two miles of carrying it, they said we weren't keeping pace and had to load it into the truck. We finally got to the Bloodroot trail, time to go up into the mountains.

Once we got to the peak, we had to crawl downhill for a few miles. Back on our feet, we then had to take off our shoes and socks. We then proceeded to hike without shoes for a mile or so. I tried being in the front of the pack. Every time we stopped, I was able to rest and take off the sandbag. Having my shoes off didn't affect me as much as some people.

When we arrived at the farm, Joe told us to leave our packs and take our sandbags. A guy who had quit the night before wanted back in. Joe had him sitting in the pond. Someone had to give up their spot for him to get back in. A few people gave up their spots, he was in unofficially.

We had to throw our sandbags in the pond, as we were told we were done with them. But then we were told to get them back out and put them back in again. This was crazy. Some people's sandbags floated on the water. While we were doing that, our bags were thrown in the creek. We had to fish them out and then go get our sandbags again. This is where having my stuff in dry bags might have helped, all my stuff was soaked. Having an extra pair of shoes and socks was worthless since they were soaked.

We had to switch two giant rocks from their original positions without ruining the grass. Some people thought we should try and lift them up, but the consensus was to try and roll them. We were given one hour and every minute over was 100 burpees. Needless to say, we racked up a lot of burpees. At the barbed wire crawl, we were told to drop our sandbags off at the fence. We had 10 minutes to low crawl through the ¼ mile barbed wire track. Nobody made it on time. I made it about 90% around the track before they pulled everyone off.

Now the group had to go back up into the mountains. A few miles in, we arrived at a cabin. We got our buckets out, some filled them half full with water. Time for some PT—pass them down the line and don't let them catch up. After that, it was time to gather some rocks from the trail. The point was to start filling buckets with rocks. After they were full, we had to head up the mountain.

When we reached a certain point, the first 25 people went through, and the rest—we learned, went up to Shrek's cabin. The 25 of us, all guys, had to cut down two trees and build a bridge across a creek. This was an interesting task since we had to find two good trees, chop them down, and place them across the ravine.

Once we were done with the trees, we had to go up to the top. The rest of the people were up there, clearing brush. We had to start helping them and clear most of it before Joe got there.

Joe gave us a little speech and told us it was burpee time. We had 3,000 to do. At that point, I was still feeling okay. We had to make a choice of which group we were going to be in, the good group or the weak group. I have never attempted 3,000 burpees in one shot so I chose the weaker group. I went until 180 and knew that if I kept going at that pace, I wasn't going to last. I made it to 220 and decided to give in. It was a hard decision but I knew I wouldn't make it much farther without getting injured.

Overall, it was a great experience. I met a lot of really cool people. It was a very difficult race and I don't think I would change anything. I made some mistakes. I gave it my all. I didn't cheat or dodge any responsibility. This race was unfair, it wasn't meant to be fair. It was designed to break you and make you quit. The farther you got, the harder it got. I'm happy about how I did and will further my training and learn from the mistakes I made.

Bonefrog Buffalo

Bonefrog was coming back to Buffalo. They were going back to Kissing Bridge. After all the races I have done, I figured I would try out their endurance option. I would do one challenge lap, then do as many sprint laps before the cutoff as possible. I wanted to push myself farther this year. This would be the perfect opportunity.

Amy, Stefanie, and I decided to volunteer with the build. It was harder for me since I worked all day. It's always nice to see how the course comes together and what is involved in making race day happen. I wouldn't be volunteering race day like I did last year but I could for build and tear down. I helped with putting up the A-Frame and a few other obstacles. Most of the course was already done by the time I volunteered and it was just getting everything in place.

On race day, there was a few of us doing *Endurance.* They told us that we had to make sure we went over the start and finish mat for each lap, easy enough. *Endurance* would start first then the tier one, challenge, and Sprint would follow. The cut-off was at 2pm to run our last lap. The goal was to keep going, don't stop. Then grab my food or water and head back. It was a hot one with the temperature in the 80s and no cloud cover.

I was having an easier time on obstacles and only failed the chopper and the balance beam. There was no completion band for non-elite runners and I don't think there were penalties for failing an obstacle on this race.

Heat was going to be a factor later on. This was at a ski resort so *Bonefrog* took full advantage of the hills. One of the biggest problems from the course last year was the course markings. A lot of people got lost and either did way more than they had to or cut the course. Since we volunteered last year and ran the volunteer wave, we didn't have too many issues with following the course. I've come to realize that races mark the course like a seasoned runner would. They fail to take into account that some people have never run a trail marked course. It's not just *Bonefrog*; it's a lot of races. Even *Spartan* has had issues.

I wanted to pace myself. I didn't want to worry about what place I was in, I would find out after the race. I had to worry about myself. As much as I wanted to be competitive, doing *Endurance* was still new to me. Overall, I kept moving at a steady pace and was at a 90% obstacle completion rate. I had to push for the final lap. I was cramping up big time and had to stop to roll my legs out. Exhaustion was hitting me hard. I just wanted to be done.

After finishing my last lap, I collapsed on the ground. The cramping was hitting me hard. Amy had the rollers trying to help me out. I was the first one done doing *Endurance*. Okay, how many laps was I behind? I guess I'll find out very soon. The rest of the team had left and there were few people left. We decided to head out. By the time we were at the car, they were doing the awards. I heard my name, hmmmm, okay— what did I win? Apparently, I had placed first in the open wave of *Endurance*. No way. This was the first time I had won first place. It kind of sucked that everyone left and not many people were there to witness it.

Spartan Killington Ultra

I had to go back. I was so close to finishing last year that I knew I could finish. The only problem was logistics. How would I pay for this trip? I was already stretched thin with the Dallas trip and *Nor-Am*, plus Amy couldn't go. I would need help. Luckily a few people from the *One Buffalo* group were going. Jim and Scott were glad to have me tag along. They were doing the *Beast* and were impressed I was going to do the *Ultra*. I would have a ride and a place to stay. I just needed a ride to the venue in the morning. Brian was doing the *Ultra* too and offered to pick me up.

This year, *Spartan* decided to change up the *Ultra Beast*, and call it the *Ultra*. Killington would be harder this year, as they added an extra loop to the *Beast* course for the *Ultra* runners.

First lap

There has to be a plan of attack going into *Killington*. I wasn't going to go into this race again with no strategy. Where I had failed before, I had trained and prepared. I was going to crush this race. I planned on finishing in less than 13 hours which seemed ambitious, I would find out if it was possible. My biggest issue last year was running downhill, I lost so much time on that. My legs couldn't take the beating of actually running downhill. I was brought to a very slow walk by the time I DNFd. I wasn't afraid of the ascents. I struggled with the *Death March* but it didn't break me. I was also better at obstacles and hopefully that would help.

I was focused, confident, and I had shown how much better I had become in those first miles.

The *Ultra* and the *Beast* split off, this would be the first taste of the extra loop. There were a few extra obstacles in this loop, but nothing difficult. The sled drag and the armor are both brute strength obstacles so I breezed through. I failed the Tarzan swing. I fell into the water and had to do my 30 burpees. After that, I didn't fail any other obstacles.

Second lap

I hit transition in just over six hours, which made a 13 hour finish time still possible. I was feeling good, nothing hurt too badly, and no blisters yet. I didn't want to change my socks or shoes; I just resupplied and headed back out. Leaving transition, I was in a much better spot than last year. I could still run downhill.

The biggest problem with multi-loop races is going out on that next loop. Pain sets in, doubt sets in, and the dread of doing that *Death March* again. Any reason not to go back out will start to fester and if you let it take root, it will derail getting out of transition.

I started out strong, I felt good.

When I hit the extra loop, there wasn't a bottleneck this time. The only problem was that I had run out of water. Was there a water station at the obstacles? I couldn't remember but I was really hoping there was. I got to the bottom and there was no water, what do I do now? It would be miles before an aid station and now I'm heading back up the steep climb. Luckily, one of the volunteers had an extra bottle of water and it got me halfway up the climb. Another runner was nice enough to give me a few sips of water so I could keep going. It would have been brutal without that water and I'm not sure how much more I could have gone.

Getting back onto the *Beast* course, we were now mixed with the *Beast* runners. One of the courtesies of *Spartan* races, while there is an *Ultra* and a *Beast* race going on is to let the *Ultra* runners pass you. "*Ultra* on the left," people would yell out as I passed by. It's a great feeling when everyone is cheering for you as you tackle this brutal course. Most runners would say they could never do the *Ultra*, but even being out on that course deserves respect. It is not easy and is dubbed one of the hardest *Spartan* races out there.

Coming back into the festival area off the last downhill, I knew I was going to finish. Nothing could stop me; the only problem was with my math. I couldn't remember when I started. How many hours had I been running? Was I going to make the 13 hour cutoff that I self-imposed? No, I was at 12 hours, or was it 14? Now I was really confused and why are my eyes watering? I don't get emotional on a course, but knowing I was going to finish plus being confused, had sent me into an emotional spiral.

The bucket carry

In the before times, as a racer, you had to fill your bucket with gravel to a certain point and then proceed to carry it in your arms. Shoulder carries were not allowed, for safety reasons. Now, *Spartan* had decided to use prefilled buckets with lids. It was to deter cheating or make it more efficient, I can't remember the reasoning.

Not only did I finish this race, but I crushed it. I finished in 13 hours and 4 minutes, just minutes over my ambitious goal. I was on top of the world and overwhelmed. Luckily, I ran into some friends and they brought me to food. I was probably a little delirious at that point. I don't even remember what I got to eat, French fries I think.

The Cryfecta

Most times I come up with my own bad ideas. This time was different. Cullen suckered me into this thing called the

Cryfecta. It was an unofficial name for doing a *Spartan Ultra*, a 12 hour *Hurricane Heat*, and the *Hurricane Heat* all in one weekend. Then we would do the *Sprint* on Sunday before our flight left. Sometimes you do hard things to see if you can do it. Sometimes you do things to be legendary. Not many people had ever attempted it, let alone completed it.

The events do not fall on the same weekend very often. This was going to be our chance. Everything seemed great on paper. We would fly in, stay at his brother's house near the airport, and get a rental to go to the venue. I was going to fly out of Cleveland since it was $300 cheaper than flying out of Buffalo. I don't know why I thought Cleveland was only two hours away, but I did. It wasn't until we were leaving that I put it into the GPS and realized the distance, that's a downer. I would have to speed to get to the airport on time. Just a little before the Ohio border, boom, a state trooper comes up behind me. I didn't deny I was speeding. I told him my situation, hoping that maybe I would get a little leniency. Nope, just add that to the things I can't afford for this trip.

I learned a valuable lesson, not to fly with a ruck plate in my carry-on. I had a very strict budget for this weekend. Every dollar mattered. Unfortunately, I had to check my plate and it cost me another $30. That hurt, but I needed my plate for the 12 hour event. I just made it through security and got on the plane minutes before takeoff. I was not in a good mood. How was this event going to go if this is what I have to deal with before it even starts? I stewed on that flight instead of letting it go. I was going to meet Cullen at the airport. He was flying out of Pittsburgh and would arrive a little before me.

Cullen found me waiting outside. He has this energy that gives you a good feeling. He was excited and I let go of the crap that had me aggravated. Bad things happen. It's how you respond to them that matters. I shouldn't have let that stuff get to me but now I could focus on getting ready. Normally, I had myself to rely on when traveling. This was completely out of my element. My family is great but very conservative. They definitely don't understand why I run. Cullen's brother was very generous; it's awesome that he's so supportive.

He had offered to take us to a massage place. Cullen and I would use the saunas, while he got a massage. This was only my second time using a sauna. They had multiple options, so we tried them all—different heats, lights, sounds, and there was even an ice sauna. At the end they had individual pools, and again, with different temperatures. I don't know if this was a rule or if I was scammed but the pools were sans bathing suits. I've come a long way.

A couple of years ago and there's no way I would have done it. But I undressed and jumped into a heated pool, then worked my way down in temperature until I got to the ice water one. In all my years of doing crazy events and stunts, I've become a firm believer in cold training. Don't be like me and just dive head first into an ice-covered pond. Do a little research and slowly build it into your routine.

Afterwards, Cullen's brother treated us to dinner. I'm pretty sure it was a local high-end steak house, or something I would normally not go to. I am a very picky eater and even more so before a big race. My go-to meal before a race is usually Texas Roadhouse and I'm shocked they don't sponsor me. I've been to almost every Texas Roadhouse on the East Coast, at least one in each state. But sometimes you have to go with the flow and appreciate the generosity of others. Another lesson I am still learning.

HH12H

We got to the venue early and ran into Ronald. Ronald is a friend that we met at the *Death Race*. He was also attempting the *Cryfecta*. We did not know it at the time, but there were two more people attempting the *Cryfecta*. The hardest part of doing something this big is realizing how big it really is and not being overwhelmed by it. Each event on its own is very difficult, but tying four events together in one weekend—insane. My mindset going into the 12 hour is to focus on the task at hand, not worry about anything else. Get through the 12 hour and worry about the *Ultra* later, when I get to it.

You are allowed one mental breakdown per event. Then you have to suck it up and keep moving. Before I started racing, there were rumors about the 12 hour and that the *Krypteia* would thin out the numbers to make the event look more difficult. From the 12 hour(s) I had done, it didn't seem to be true. Maybe I got lucky and had good leaders. I just had to focus on what Cullen and I were doing. We were in this together and had to have each other's back if we were going to finish this.

We had to fill our two sandbags ¾ full of gravel and bring them back. This would be for another task. We left them at our base camp and headed over to the lake.

We had to carry a tarp filled with water as a team. There were three teams. We weren't on the same team. It's okay. There will be times when we won't be on the same team. The 12 hour is a team and an individual event. After we filled the tarp, we had to carry it up what seemed like the only hill in Texas. I thought Texas was flat, this is ridiculous.

There was a small footpath to the top, but it was difficult. It was dark by the time we reached the top and now we had to get back down. My team was pretty good. We got the job done with minimal complaining. There were times when the water would slosh towards the low points making it difficult to hold. That's where teamwork and communication played in. If we didn't talk, half the team suffered.

Since the sun had gone down, the heat wasn't as bad. It was still hot compared to what I'm used to, but manageable. One thing I didn't take into consideration was the rain storms that had hit days before. We found out later that parts of the course were flooded and super muddy.

We had to run the course with our sandbag, ruck to a point on the course, and come back. The sandbag wasn't too heavy so we flew through the course. Our next task was to navigate the course with our sandbag and fill our bucket up with water. I believe there were hole- punches that we had to find at obstacles and punch out on our card.

Run the course with double sandbags? This was going to be tough. It wasn't too bad before but now we were tired. When your friend is starting to show signs of cracking, you have to step in and help out. The only way we are finishing this is together. Remember— one task at a time, one event at a time. We regrouped and completed the task in the top10.

We went to the edge of a golf course. Each ball that we found would knock down the burpees we had accumulated. We had all spread out and tried to grab as many as we could. It was fairly difficult to find golf balls in the dark but we had a giant pile at the end.

At the end of the event, we walked over to the gun range where Chris Kyle and Chad Littlefield were murdered in 2013. I won't go into the backstop but it was a very emotional speech that was given. For me, it gave me the motivation to get through the rest of the weekend. We were given a bracelet made of Paracord. I still have it with my dog tag for finishing.

Ultra

During the HH12H, I convinced Cullen to run with me at the 7 am open wave. He was registered to run Age Group at 6:30 am. One of the worst ideas was running open. I cut my time to complete it by an hour, making a nearly impossible task that much harder. After we got to the corral—dropping my Walmart bag of a roller, a bag of *Sour Patch Kids*, and a grape *Powerade*—Joe Desena decided to give a speech further pushing our start time back.

I definitely started to panic, each precious minute that passed, meant I had even less of a margin for error. I don't know why I had it in my head that the *Hurricane Heat* started at 5 o'clock pm. I thought I had more time. Since we knew how muddy the course was, and how few dry spots there were, we had to run as much as possible. Running this fresh would have been tough, running this after a brutal 12 hour *Hurricane Heat* was a whole new level of suck. There was an artificial time limit for finishing before the start of the *Hurricane Heat*. Starting in the last *Ultra* wave made this nearly impossible. I've only run an *Ultra* with Amy. That didn't turn out so well and that was fresh. We were now 14 hours from the start of the last event and things were going to get rough.

The course was still muddy and looked much different in the light. We had adrenaline flowing from being with a brand new group of people. I was concerned about the heat of the midday sun that would cook us later. The course had very little shade. I was worried about snakes and other critters. Hopefully, with enough people making noise, it would deter them from being on the path. The obstacles were standard for a *Spartan Ultra* and we railed out the first lap in plenty of time. I think I only failed two obstacles overall.

Transition

We finished the first lap and I was feeling pretty good. We had to keep this short and sweet. I refilled my water bottle, had a few sour patch kids, and then we headed back out after I rolled out for a few minutes. Things were looking good time wise. It took us 4 hours and 15 minutes to do the first lap. The course was drying out. We had to keep a good pace in order to finish before the start of the *Hurricane Heat.* I also had to worry about slowing down once it was hot out again.

Lap 2

We started out great. Now we were mixed in with the *Beast* runners. One problem I forgot about was bottlenecks at the obstacles. With more runners on the course, certain spots were prone to backups. It didn't matter how fast we were if we couldn't move through people. I never thought we would pass *Beast* runners like they were standing still. We were hauling. We were both still feeling great. Obstacles were getting more difficult but we still hadn't failed any yet.

HH

For some reason we thought it started at 5pm, so we got some food and got our buckles. As we were walking over, we saw that we were late. We ran over and joined the PT. I was drained, just completely run down and this was killing me. It almost felt like my body weighed 400 lbs, every moment was difficult. I was starting to get dizzy and was almost at my breaking point. Keep pushing, I kept telling myself.

There was another guy struggling. We kept trying to encourage him and keep him going. I was on autopilot and honestly can't remember much of the running back and forth. Some low crawls, bear crawls, sprints, and just general suck. What was supposed to be the easiest event—turned out to be a quest to keep pushing forward when all I wanted to do was pass out. We walked over to the festival area and had to low crawl through the mud. We had to do some embarrassing task like singing or dancing in front of the crowd. It's nice having support when you're at your worst.

We had to fill our ammo can with gravel and then write down something that weighed us down. The paper was placed inside our ammo can and we had to fill it with gravel. This was our burden for the rest of the race.

At one point we were wrist-tied to a partner and had to move as a team up and down mud hills. I was teamed up with a friend that I had worked with before so we did pretty good.

We ended the *Hurricane Heat* and I had made some new friends, with five of us completing all three events together. Nothing brings you closer than doing something as crazy as this.

Sprint

Rob let us stay at his hotel after the *Hurricane Heat*. I slept on the floor after taking a shower. Rob was a savior and had chocolate milk, the lifeblood. We showed up that morning, hoping to get into a corral. We made it in and took it fairly easy. It was super muddy. I couldn't complete the slip wall at the end, the first time it. We walked around in shame for a few minutes, but we were legends—*Quadfecta* complete. I remember Cullen's knee buckled, either between the wall or the fire jump, but he finished.

It was time to get cleaned up before our flights left. We had to clean our rucks so they didn't smell like death on the plane.

Cullen dropped me off before heading to his gate. I still had to take a bus to my terminal. This was going to be close. I made it to the check-in and I had about 20 minutes to make it to my gate. I didn't have time to check my bags so everything had to go with me.

Imagine doing the hardest race up to this point, only having a couple of hours of sleep, and trying to carry all your stuff through the airport. I still had my plate and ruck plus my luggage. I couldn't afford to miss my flight. I dug deep and ran as fast as possible through the airport. When you are in a rush, the gate is never close. Everything hurt. I was going on what little adrenaline I had left.

I made it, with no time to spare. I could finally rest. I didn't have the strength to put my ruck in the overhead compartment. It was probably better that way especially with the plate. This crazy adventure was finally coming to an end. The last thought I had before I fell asleep on the plane was thank goodness I didn't have to pay for my ruck plate again.

5

2019

Planning for 2019 would be an incredible task. I wanted to do my first 100 miler, a *GORUCK STAR* course, my first *GORUCK HTL*, *GORUCK* Team Assessment and Selection. It was ambitious and it was getting bigger with every event I added: *Death Race*, another *HTL*, a second *STAR* course, *Bonefrog Trident*, and *Indian Mud Run*. This was going to be a big year. I didn't know how big it would turn out to be. It was almost like the *Cryfecta*, in which this was a made-up thing I was doing.

It was my year of endurance. I would do the hardest events in the United States, back to back, until I finished them all or died in the process. Had anyone even tried to accomplish this? I had known of people trying for the World Record of 100 milers in a year, and I would meet one of them at the *Beast of Burden* later that year. This would take skill as a runner, mental fortitude for the multi-day events, and strength for carrying weight/ doing obstacles. I couldn't be one-dimensional; I had to be the whole package if I wanted to do this. Just training for a 100 miler is time consuming. I could break down how training for any of these is usually a lifetime achievement for normal people. Ask anyone you know if they ever ran an ultra marathon. Then ask them if they did it with weight, you might get one person.

I don't say this to brag but to put this into perspective. Anything I did wasn't because I'm some super athlete who trained for years and had some secret way to finish. Running 100 miles is more of a mental test than a physical one. Some people do not care to try to run ultras. I completely understand. Just like anything in life, some things bring more people joy than other things. I find my peace in doing these events and pushing myself. There are days and times when this is torture and I have to drag myself to do it. Don't think that any of this was easy for me, at almost every event I had to question why I wanted to finish. I will give a brief description of what certain events entailed so everyone has a basic idea of what they were about.

Beast of Burden 100 Winter

This was my first time attempting a 100 mile ultra marathon. My goal for 2019 is to get the 200 mile buckle for the Beast of Burden, by finishing the winter and summer 100 milers. This was the 10 year anniversary and there was a custom buckle commemorating the special occasion. That buckle was going to be mine. It was like icing on the cake, that extra incentive to sign up and finish.

Training

My longest training run going into this race was just under 27 miles with a 30lb ruck. I did a lot of short runs, and tried to do them as late as possible, when I was exhausted. My cold training, running in shorts and no shirt would get me adapted to the cold. I think rucking and doing the Cryfecta definitely helped with keeping motivated for the longer hours.

First 25 miles

I wanted to do the first 25 mile loop fasted. I prepared for the cold, but made sure to overdress and wore a long sleeve shirt and wind breaker. I wore my Altra IQ road shoes with darn tough socks. Most people had hydration packs, I used a hip belt with a bottle filled with Powerade zero. I felt great running, and ran to the first aid station with Seb and Heather. Average pace to the turnaround was just under an 11 min mile. I was trying not to go out too fast, but I couldn't slow down my pace enough.

25-50

At the start point, mile 25, I switched to my Altra Lone Peak 4.0, and doubled my socks up to provide more cushion. I had a ham wrap and refilled my bottle. I had 4 of my Anti-fatigue Hammer pills and headed out after stretching and rolling.

By the turnaround, mile 37.5, I had a cappuccino (non-keto) and mozzarella sticks. By the time I hit the Gasport aid station, mile 43, it was not sitting right and that slowed me down and was my first bathroom break.

50-75

I started to eat carbs and candy at this leg of the race. I still felt really good and was able to consistently run, I did add in some run/walk at this point. My body was starting to get tired but the cold was keeping me awake and out of pain.

75-100

Amy was going to pace me for the final 25 miles. At this point, I wasn't sure how much more I could run, walking would still guarantee me a finish, but would take a lot longer. After the Gasport aid station, mile 82, my right knee started to ache. I had calf compression sleeves on both legs, and when we hit the

Middleport aid station, I moved the right sleeve up to my knee to give it more support. It seemed to work and I was able to run a little more.

At the Middleport aid station, I saw Billy Richards there, I asked him for some advice on doing the Ultras, and told him he was an inspiration. We took off before he did, but he caught up to us a few miles out. He let us run/walk with him to Gasport and it definitely helped me mentally, and gave me a push to finish strong.

I finished with a time of 26 hours 15 minutes and 32 seconds. I felt pretty good after, tired and sore, but nothing like I was after doing the 50 miler last year. My goal was to finish, but I pushed hard and finished strong and crushed my original goal.

Columbus Star Course

This is one of those events I swear I would never do again. It seemed easy enough, just 50 miles with a 20lb ruck. I signed up not knowing I needed a team. I had an event code for being our local group ruck leader so the only expense would be going down and possibly a hotel. I needed someone to go along with me. There wasn't much interest in our ruck group for doing a 50 mile ruck. Seb was still traumatized by the *DC 50* miler he did last year. Luckily for me, there was a discussion on the event page with people looking for teammates. Rob needed a partner, so it was perfect. A few weeks before the event, Amy decided she wanted to do it as well. If you are going for time in a star course, the more people you have, the more issues can arise. We weren't going for time, just to finish.

The *GORUCK* star course is not like other *GORUCK* events. There is no PT, no yelling, and no sandbags/coupons. This is just straight-up rucking. There are multiple options for distances. I wanted to do the 50 miler. The concept is to navigate waypoints in order to complete the course in as little distance as possible. The shortest course would be 50 miles and if you went out of your way, well...bonus miles.

This is a team event and you would have to start out as a team of two minimum but it was possible to finish solo. There were prizes for coming in the top three but you had to finish as a team to qualify. At the start of the event, your team leader is given a list of waypoints and instructions on what to take pictures of when you arrive. The entire team has to be in the picture and it had to be uploaded to *Instagram*, with the correct hashtag for each waypoint. This was not just running 50 miles with a 20lb ruck. You also have a 20lb plate if you are over 150lb or a 10lb plate if you are less than 150lb. Stopping is allowed, you can go into stores or restaurants and bars if you so choose, you have 20 hours to finish.

We got down to Columbus early and stopped to get some dinner before the event started.

I was chosen to be our leader and would get our paper with our points after we weighed in our rucks. The time starts after you get your points, not when you leave. The more time you take to plot your course, the less time you have to ruck. We decided to use two phones to navigate, one would use the *Road warrior* app to plot all the points so we could see the order we needed to go in. The other phone would use *Google Maps* go get us to each point. We tried marking them in the paper in the order we were going to do them and check them off as we completed them. That would come in handy so we didn't miss one.

I felt like we had to go at a faster pace in early part of the event because we would eventually slow down. I was hoping we could do a 13–14 minute mile, to build a buffer for stopping. I tried to account for bathroom breaks, stretching, foot care, and food. The one thing I didn't factor in was what areas were better in the daytime versus overnight. I had planned for us to rail out the closest points early, hit the longest point towards the end, and then head back to a few more points.

We hit most of the close points and Amy wanted us to slow down. We were close to a 16–17 minute mile at that point. It wasn't bad but I wanted to keep moving a little faster. Was it the best idea? I'm not sure because at mile 25, Amy was done. Her feet were toast. Would having gone slower helped or was she doomed from the beginning? She called for a ride to the start and Rob and I were off on our way. We were off to the furthest point, the dam. Our pace was a lot faster for a few miles, but it didn't last. Rob was slowing down now. We were still moving at a good pace but I think he was hurting.

After we hit the dam, we put in the next waypoint. This is where double checking addresses is important. There were two streets with the same name, with the same numbers but in different towns. Ironically, almost the same distance away, but in opposite directions. I messed up badly. When we got close to the address, we realized it wasn't right. At this point, Rob was done. Amy came to get him. She brought me back on course. A few miles from the waypoint, I was now over 10 miles away. I had to call the cadre and tell them I was going solo now. I had to check in every hour now to ensure that I was okay.

I made it back to civilization, I started seeing other teams. It was starting to get warm out.

Philly HTL

This was my only planned *GORUCK HTL* for 2019. It turned out to be the most unplanned event I've ever done. Any planning I did fell apart before, during, and after the event. How I finished this one is still a miracle, not one thing went right.

Seb and I planned on doing this one together. He had two friends who were also doing the *HTL*. We would all chip in on a hotel near the start. Sounds like a great plan, right? Seb would later get injured and defer the event. No big deal, I would still have two people to rely on to get through this. Nope, the day before I would learn I was on my own and needed to get my own hotel. I wasn't upset that the plan had changed. It would have been awkward to share a hotel room with two girls I had just met. I was more upset that I found out the day before and had no way to get a hotel room anywhere near the start line. It wasn't in the budget— change of plans, now I had no where to go in between the events. If I park in a ramp and use that as a base, it might work. I planned to sleep in the bed of my truck to rest between events.

On my way to Philadelphia, I stopped at a running store to get a few supplies. I thought I should stock up on gel packs. I found a pair of underwear that supposedly was designed to not ride up. Perfect, I've been looking for a good pair of undies for a while now. I stopped at a grocery store to pick up a few more things, mostly for dinner beforehand. It was a nice place to stop and take a nap before the event began.

I parked in a ramp just a few blocks from where the event would start. I had a bit of time so decided to head over and see who was there. It would give me time to stretch and calm my nerves.

The Heavy

This was going to be a rough one, the temperature would be

the hottest it's been all year. We were going to start this class with 23 people. The majority of the group was going for the *Bolts*, which are earned after completing all three events in one weekend.

Finding water

Our first team challenge was to fill up our water bags. We were in downtown Philadelphia so it shouldn't be that hard.

PT in the Water Fountain

There is nothing like starting an event soaking wet. Not only did it downpour, we got to do PT in a giant water fountain with onlookers. One thing I learned from doing crazy stuff before is that drain holes are a lifesaver. When we went into the water, the ruck would fill up with water. We would have to overhead press it. Thirty pounds and a bag full of water was difficult but if you let the water drain beforehand, it wasn't as bad. The girl next to me was having a really hard time. She wasn't letting the water out of her bag before she would try to lift it. I showed her to unzip it a little bit and flip it over before lifting it up. Now she wasn't struggling as bad. This is a team event and you want to help as many people finish as possible. One, it's the right thing to do, and two, you need bodies to help carry the load. The sandbags get heavier when you can't switch them with other people.

The 12 mile timed ruck

We were in a shady area of Philadelphia. We were told to stick with someone with a phone for this part. I had my phone in the truck so I would have to stick with someone. We had 3 ½ hours to complete the ruck. I planned on doing it faster and having some time to rest and eat. The path was an out and back and we would have to do it twice to get 12 miles in.

The Deck of Cards

Cadre Cleve is well known for his deck of cards workout and this would be my first time experiencing it. Each suite was a different type of workout and each card was the reps you had to do. The jokers were a short run around a tree and back. We started at 6–7am so it wasn't super hot out yet but it felt really hot. This was the first time I had struggled with the heat and I wasn't the only one. I couldn't stop sweating and each exercise was getting more difficult. I couldn't drink enough and if this didn't stop soon, I really thought I would pass out. Before I had the chance to drop out, another person had succumbed to the heat. Thank goodness we get to stop for a little bit was all I could think about. Thinking back that sounds kind of mean. Once I came to my senses though, I felt sympathy for the person. There was very little shade.

The chaffing

These had to be the worst pair of underwear I had ever worn for an event. Not even 12 hours into the heavy and the chaffing was so bad I couldn't walk right anymore. My inner thighs were raw. I didn't know how much more I could take. Each step was excruciating. I kept trying to adjust so I could get some comfort but it would only last a few steps. I didn't know what to do. It was halfway through the first event. I had two more days to go. Ever come up with a terrible idea that works out? Well this one was outside the box. I knew it would be painful but it might bring relief now. I had a roll of duct tape. You are probably cringing thinking of what I was about to do. I duct taped my leg from my crotch to about halfway down my thigh on each leg. Would it work or was it just a painful waste of time? I had to do something. I would find out if it was the right choice fairly soon.

The Tough

Rough Start (flag down)

There was no time to sleep. Lying down was a bad idea. I had no one to rely on to wake me up in time for the *Tough*. I would stop at Starbucks and get some caffeine. I like those coffee bullshit things and really don't know how to order them, but I tried. I was trying not to get a sugary drink since I would crash in a little bit. It was some Frankenstein creation of coffee, heavy cream, and ice with maybe a hint of vanilla. It was gross but I sucked it down. I just had to restock my ruck and I would be good. I always bring *Sour Patch Kids* as an emergency snack. It's that one treat that will snap me out of a bad time. I also had more *Bloc* energy chews, easy to eat caffeine on the go. I figured at some point I would be completely exhausted and would need every trick in the book to get through this. I was running on four hours of sleep in the past 36 hours.

We showed up to the start of the *Tough* and we were going to start with the welcome party. The flag carrier set the flag on the ground which is the biggest mistake you can make in an event. I wanted to walk away because this was only going to get worse. Cadre Cleve noticed the transgression. We were going to be in for a bad time. I wanted to run to the truck and take a nap because if this is how we are starting the *Tough*, there's no hope. Our punishment was 30 burpees but we had to do them in sync. So those 30 burpees turned into a couple hundred. We would get a few in, back down to one. Did we really do them in sync, did it matter? Just keep doing them until he says stop, that's all I could think.

Kat

Kat had done a few events in Buffalo and she was the only familiar face I saw during this weekend. I had forgotten that she was going to be there and she is a beast during events.

The Struggle to stay awake

When we entered the baseball field with all the sandbags, Cadre Belman had a fun exercise to do. I think it was nicknamed the "Pain Train." We had to connect the sandbags together and break them up into multiple teams. The concept was to move them as a team across the field. I was fading fast. I couldn't keep my eyes open, each movement felt like I was in quicksand neck deep. I just wanted to close my eyes for a few moments. The concept is called a micro nap (or micro sleep) and basically, you either pass out or fall asleep for a few seconds or a few minutes. After we were done with the exercise, Cadre Belman was talking. We were not allowed to close our eyes or fall asleep. I may have dozed off for a few seconds but definitely passed out when we were ready to move out. It was only for a few minutes but it gave me some energy back. I wasn't 100% but I could function again.

Soon we were on the path that we did the 12 mile timed ruck on. It looked a lot different in daylight. It was time for Cadre Cleve's deck of cards. It wasn't as hot this time and our exercises weren't as difficult, so that made it easier. After so much physical activity, my body was just numb to the movements. It was almost like being on autopilot, like an out-of-body experience. Is this really happening, am I being tortured, or is this just a dream? I don't remember being in pain, at least not as bad as the *Heavy.*

The Light

The start of the *Light* was at a different location than the *Heavy* and *Tough* so I would need to find a ride. Luckily, Kat was willing to help me out. I was beyond exhausted and there still wasn't time for sleep. I was starting to get cranky but I had one more event to get through. There is a concept during these events where you hide in the big group of people and just sail through. It wasn't possible in the *Buffalo HTL* because there were three of us that they knew were doing it. The sandbags were still the same weight but we had three times as many people to carry them now. These people were fresh and the five of us who had made it to the *Light* were not.

Some of the people who had done the *Heavy* but didn't show up for the *Light* were back, so were those girls. Now it was, I am going to finish this, and I'm going to kick ass. No hiding, I'll carry a sandbag the entire time just to prove a point. Not sure what the point is but I'll prove it. My brain couldn't think logically and maybe that was for the best. I just had to finish.

Those Sandbags

Cadre Belman brought out the "Pain Train" exercise again. Oh joy. The one girl said that this was a cool idea and I said you should've been here last night. I said it in the most snarkiest and loud way possible. I did say that I was cranky before this started, justified no, but it made me feel better at the time. Am I sorry, absolutely, but it took me a few days to realize it.

Some PT

The Home Stretch

We just had to get back to the start point and boom, this nightmare would be over. We had to walk the same path as the *Tough*. I remember carrying that sandbag by myself. It felt like forever to get back to the start. We made it back. It was now time to line up and get those coveted patches. The Cadre started with the *Light* patches and once everyone got one, it was time for the *HTL* patches and Cadre patches. If you did a certain amount of events with a Cadre, you earned one of their special patches.

Death Race

After the 2018 *Death Race*, I vowed never to do the *Death Race* again. There was no need. I wasn't going to put myself through the games and stupidity. When it was announced for 2019, I didn't sign up right away. The rules came out after a while that you needed a partner. It couldn't be anyone that was already signed up. That itch to go back was starting to form. No one would want to partner with me. My buddy, Amanda, who had done the *Cryfecta* with me, needed a partner. She was a badass but had only ever done a 12 hour *Hurricane Heat*. Would that matter? Our height and weight differences might cause trouble if we had to work together. It would be easy if I had to buddy carry her but the *Death Race* is never about making things easy. Paying for the race was also a concern. I needed a miracle if I going to sign up.

Heading to Vermont

I'll do a rundown of my gear list for the event:

- Ruck—Last year, I used the *Rucker* and I didn't have enough room. I made it work but I thought this year I would upgrade to the *GR1*. I went minimalist with gear to ensure that everything I had, I would need.
- Bucket—I swore I wouldn't bring a bucket again, but it's a necessary evil. It did come in handy, and it's not the *Death*

Race unless you bring a bucket. If I ever do the *Death Race* again, I would find a better way to secure it to my Ruck.

· Axe—After last year's debacle with my axe breaking two swings in, I went with a *Fisker* axe practiced with it.
· Paracord—I had some bundled up, Amanda also gave me some looped up. We measured and marked a few distances on it in case we needed to know a specific measurement. It's one of those things that doesn't take up extra space but can come in handy.
· Folding saw—This was on the mandatory gear list.
· Two cans of food.
· $20 bill note.
· Compass.
· Sound Proof earplugs.
· Construction ear muffs.
· Blindfold.
· Sewing Kit.
· Cloth, in a floral print.
· Duct tape (not silver).
· Ten balloons.
· Bag balm.
· One Dart.
· Water Sanitizer (your choice).
· Whistle.
· Chemlights (3 red, 3 green).
· Ten pack of 11" Zip ties (Black).
· Shovel—On the mandatory gear list.
· Chopstick/toothpick—on the mandatory gear list.
· Tinfoil—a two square foot piece that had no wrinkles or folds.

Random things that I brought to help out:

- PVC pipe (to protect the tinfoil).
- Extra socks.
- Trekking poles.
- Dry bags.
- Carabineers.
- Sharpie marker.
- Homemade fire starting kit (a mix of cotton, lint, wax, sawdust, and magnesium.
- Multi-tool, it never hurts to have one.

The Documentary

It was advised that we should attend the preview of the 2018 *Death Race* documentary the night before. Was this a trap? Would the Death Race start early? Amanda and I thought about bringing our gear just in case but decided against it. There had been times it has started early, without anyone realizing. It was a great get-together meeting old friends and seeing new people ready to embark on this life-changing event. I was shown a few times in the documentary, mostly in the background. This was motivational. It gave me the boost of confidence I needed.

Back to the hotel and one more gear check before bed. We woke up and headed to the General Store for breakfast. I've been told that it's good to stay away from there before the *Death Race* start, but it's the closest place to our hotel.

Day 1

Don't be the first one to show up, also don't be the last. This is not a normal race, and just showing up can be punishment. When we pulled in, we were directed to park in the field. We had Amanda's rental. After she dropped me off to park the car, everyone had to pile their gear and form a gear-pyramid. I should have secured my axe a little better to my ruck, as it became separated. All the participants lined up. We were handed a bead and told not to lose it.

When we registered, we had to get our individual picture taken. We had to hand in our two cans, the $20 bill, and our envelope. They gave us a sweater and t-shirt, some people kept them and some people put them in their vehicles. Which one was the right choice, we would find out. We kept ours in our buckets.

We start our PT

First thing is gear check. Every participant lines up and we have to bear crawl to the tree line and back. If you kept your shirt, you were blindfolded and had to do PT, while holding hands of the person next to you. If you did not keep your shirt, you had to go get it and then chop wood. After all of that, we had to cut our bib number out of fabric and sew it to our bib. Easy enough, but you didn't have your ruck, you had someone else's. So you had to find their scissors and sewing kit. I struggled to get it sewn quickly, it was on there but it wasn't pretty.

Next step was low crawling to the pond. The race directors did not waste any time getting our stuff wet. Jump in, get wet, and run back. It pays not to be last. Some people were punished with carrying a log. I was fortunate and was close to the front of the pack. The broom was introduced close to this point for the last place person. If you had the broom two times in a row, you were done. I vowed to make sure that never happened.

When Joe shows up, it's never a good thing. It felt like an impossible task to get some fake punishment when we were probably going to do it anyway. This task was to memorize everyone's name. You had two minutes. The point of the task was to invoke fear. Most people shut down when something stressful happens. Luckily, we had a few people that stepped up with the idea to write your name on your bib. When you were called to say the name, it made it a lot easier to find out the person's name.

The *Death Race* has rules, but you can bend the rules just enough to finish the task. The goal of the *Death Race* is to push you out of your comfort zone so much that you quit. Not this time, I wasn't going to quit. They were going to have to send me home this time. I was fighting for more this time. I had told Kimball that I would bring back a skull for him. I was going to do everything in my power to do it.

Our next task was to head up to Shrek's cabin and come back. There was a course sweeper and if she caught up to you, you were eliminated. I didn't have the extra weight of the log and I was still fresh, so I stayed up near the front half of the runners. Once we made it back, we had to low crawl back to the pond, but this time, pushing our packs. The next task was removing two trees out of the pond to the other side of the property. We had two trees split up between us and now came the log PT. Staying in the squat position with the tree was probably the worst part.

Now we were being split into three groups, each with its own task. I went to clean the pond and Amanda went to do the steps. I had my trusty folding saw. I was plugging along until I sliced my thumb, not with the saw, but by pulling a weed out. Are you kidding me? Of course, it was deep. Luckily, I had the duct tape and bandaged myself up. Keep going—it's only a cut. Our group railed out cleaning the pond and we were the first group done. Now we had to help chop up the tree that we carried over with that group.

Some people were chopping. Others were carrying wood to the cabin. I was chopping for a little bit but then realized we needed to move the wood faster. Grab as much as you can in your hands and head up. There was a group that was using a tarp to carry the wood. We were now given a time limit and every minute we were over, equaled 100 burpees. The threat of burpees brought me back to when I quit last year. I had prepared for doing burpees until I passed out, burpees weren't going to scare me away again.

Now we had to hold hands and lunge across the field in sync. It took a few tries and finally, someone took control and got the group to work together. The final thing was doing a backward somersault with our arms locked. After we were done, our penalty was added up, magically, it was 3000 burpees. If anyone quit now, the entire group would be saved from doing burpees. An interesting offer, but no one took it. Bring it on, I'm ready. They said it would be later in the event. We had that threat hanging over our heads.

Every person was given a raw egg to hold onto until the end of the event. If it cracked, you were done. I put my egg in my sweater and wrapped it and put it in my bucket. The next task was to line up across from your partner, then move three to the right. The person across from you is your new partner. Now for the new rule—if your original partner DNFs you DNF. The new partner is yours until the end of the event. Every person was given a raw egg to hold onto until the end of the event. If it cracked, you were done. I put my egg in my sweater and wrapped it and put it in my bucket.

Was this a good thing or a bad thing? I was paired with Jeff. Was this an upgrade or a downgrade? I would find out soon. Jeff had done an *Agoge*, and multiple endurance events. The only problem is it doesn't matter what you've done, only what is happening now. We were tied together and had to move up the mountain as a team. Jeff was having issues keeping pace with everyone else. We were falling behind. Michelle, who was the sweeper, was now walking with us.

I did not want to DNF this early in the race, especially because I was paired with a weaker partner. I did everything I could to help Jeff push through. I can be motivational but have to watch out and not be too pushy.

We had the sweeper with us—walking with us and giving us advice as we moved along. It was already night time when we headed up. I didn't have my watch. There was no way to tell the time.

Our next task was to solve riddles. At each station, there was a random riddle that you had to figure out, head back down to the cabin and tell the Krypteia. If you got it right, you moved farther up the mountain to the next one. Each time you went up, there was a different way, such as low crawl and lunges. We were still zip-tied together and the tie was starting to bruise our wrists. This was a nice opportunity to micronap. After solving a riddle, we would go off to the side and close our eyes for a few minutes.

When we finally got to the last riddle, it was one of the most difficult. We tried talking to a few of my friends to see if they could figure it out. None of the people I talked to figured it out. We found out later that the answer was to bring a bucket full of water back or something silly like that. Unlike the other riddles where there was a clear answer, the final one was a task. This is where you have to think outside the box.

After about a dozen puzzles, we were told to head back to the farm. The morning sun was starting to come up. I made it through the first day. Last year, I had only made it 24 hours. My goal was to finish so getting past 24 hours was my first goal.

Our next task was land navigation. We were broken up into six teams. We had until 11am to earn 180 points from the different locations. Each location had a different value but one location was worth 180 points alone. The problem was that it was the *Bloodroot* trail and to earn the points, you had to recite a poem on one of the tombstones. Go big or go home. Our group agreed that this was our best shot. After some deliberation, we decided to send our two fastest people ahead to find the poem and write it down. The rest of the group would follow behind. We had to be a group when we recited the poem but the checkpoint for the task was not at the top of the trail.

Think smarter. Once we met back up, I came up with the idea

of each person writing a sentence from the poem on their arm. There was no rule that we all had to memorize the entire thing. It worked out in our favor and as a group we only messed up one word. The penalty was burpees.

After that, we were allowed to go to the top of the trail again, meet the camera crew and find out what fun was waiting for us. We had to show our egg to prove that we still had it. If we wanted to stay in the race, we had to eat the egg, shell and all. I hate eggs, especially raw. The only time eggs are good is when they are in cookies or cake. Well, I've done worse things, so just swish it down with water and hope I don't throw up. The weirdest part was being filmed doing it. They checked to make sure you actually swallowed it. That was incredibly gross, but I did it.

The next task was finding one of three mushrooms. I teamed up with two other people to increase our odds of finding it. Remember how there is leeway in the rules? Well, we went and searched all over for those mushrooms. People were running down to the next task as we were frantically searching. How were they finding them? This was getting frustrating. We were going up and down the trail, running through the woods, and still nothing. Now everyone was heading down and finally someone told us to grab one of the display mushrooms.

Now we had to make up time. Don't be last. All three of us were running down the mountain to our next task.

We made it down and found out our next task was making a fire. After we built the fire, we had to boil water and make a mushroom tea with the mushroom we found. Easy enough.

I had my fire starting kit. I teamed up with a guy who was struggling to make a fire. We got the fire going. He had a cup we could boil the water in. We had to make two separate fires. As luck would have it, if the fire was moved over, it counted as a different fire.

We both passed and were last to move on. Everyone else was cut. We made it through by seconds. Another bead was earned. Now it was apparent that the beads were going to spell something.

We moved on and had to run through the creek. We had to find a rock for the next task. If you picked one that was too small, you had to pick again. I got a decent sized rock; some might consider this a boulder. Now we had to get in on our backs and hold the rock up. The last person to not drop their rock was the winner. I was in the middle of the pack again, and my arms finally gave out. The winner earned someone else to carry their pack. As a group, we handed it off so it wasn't just one person carrying it. Somehow, I ended up with it for a while.

When we got closer to the farm, we got to our new task. We had to submerge in the creek for a few seconds all together. Whatever amount of time it was, we couldn't get it right so we had to keep doing it. The water felt great to me but it was cold to others.

After that, we got a break to eat, change socks, and get ready for our next movement back to the farm.

    Since we broke up into land navigation teams, I had not seen Amanda. I wasn't sure if she was still in or if she had DNF'd. I knew she was a fighter so I had figured she was still in. That was until they told us that this was all that was left for entrants. But if she DNFd, how was I still in, and Jeff wasn't there either. Well, there goes that rule.

When we got back to the farm, we met up with the people that DNF'd but had earned their way back into the race. Amanda was a part of the group but Jeff was not there. There was another break before our next task. We had to head back up the mountain to Shrek's cabin. I talked to Amanda and got updated on what had happened while telling her everything that happened to me. Now it was time to head to Miguel's cabin, following the trail they told us to. While walking as a group, we ran into a runner who was disoriented and was looking for her ruck. Amanda stepped up and helped her out. It didn't take her long to find it. It goes to show that if someone is in need of help, even if you're exhausted, you need to help out. It's the right thing to do.

Our next task was to memorize a *Lego* block configuration and head back up to Shrek's cabin and rebuild it. You could work as teams, which most people did. If you got it wrong, you had to do 250 burpees, head back down and do it again. As a group, we failed multiple times. We never got it right before our time expired. Less than a dozen people got it right. At that point, about a third of us were left. We now had to go back down to the barn for our next task.

We entered the barn and had to line up. It was story time. We had to put on our blindfolds and stand while we listened. Do not fall asleep. Pay attention, we were going to be tested and if you failed—you were done. The struggle was there. I could feel my body swaying. I heard a loud thump, someone had fallen over.

The shock of the noise was enough to startle me awake. Focus, pay attention. The story was over and now our task was to sit in silence with our blindfold and earmuffs for one hour.

We had to stand up when we thought it was an hour. If we were off, either early or late, we would be punished. As I reached for my blindfold and earmuffs, I realized that my earmuffs were gone. Now what do I do? I had to use my insole from my shoe as a makeshift earmuff. The bonus was that I could still hear what was going on around me. Unfortunately, the smell was terrible but kept me awake. I was off about two minutes on my guess. As everyone was getting done, we were about to head outside and find out our punishment. It was the combination of everyone that was off, not just your time.

Our punishment was to crawl across the field, first without using our arms, and on the way back, we couldn't use our legs. We had to do eight count bodybuilders, a form of burpee with an extra move. These were staggered. Each motion was given a number 1–8. Doing one bodybuilder wasn't just going from one through eight, there would be 1, 2, 3, back to 2, 3, 4, back to 3—so one bodybuilder took a few minutes to do.

We had to go back inside after doing five bodybuilders and take our exam. Panic was starting to build. I felt I had completely forgotten everything the story was about. This test was just a few questions and the last question stuck out. It basically stated why you should be the hero of your journey. That hit hard. Why was I the hero? Not many people think of why they do the things they do. Up until that point, I hadn't given it much thought. I like to think I'm a good person who makes a few mistakes, but in the grand scheme, I want to help people. The entire reason I was there was to help Amanda finish. Also, to prove to anyone watching my journey, that anything is possible if you put effort into it. How many hours had I been going? How many were left? Did it matter anymore? I had to keep going.

Now it was time to go back outside for some "relaxing" yoga and PT holds. Nothing about that was fun or relaxing. I hate yoga. I am not flexible at all. After we were done, trash was found where we were doing our crawls. I think the term "filthy pigs" was used to describe our group. We now had to be tied together as a group and roll/ crawl through the mud that they had created especially for us.

It was time to find our packs that were somewhere on the property but not in a building or in the woods. Someone from the group found them in a box truck and we hurried to get them out. We had to find our shoes. I went with a small group and we found them up in a tree. The other shoe we had to earn back by giving up one of our shoe laces and tying them all into a knot. I had to use duct tape and Paracord to makeshift a way to keep my shoe on for the remainder of the event.

It was starting to downpour and our next punishment was to sit underneath the awning of the brown barn while the rain and runoff soaked us. Now that we were wet, our next task was to plant seeds in the field with toothpicks and chop sticks. Our hands and fingers were not allowed to touch the seeds. I didn't mind the rain but was definitely starting to get cold. The rain was draining the heat from my body, and with little food, I could feel my body starting to shut down. Luckily, someone handed me a poncho to keep me from getting even wetter. I could feel my eyes closing. As I was kneeling down to plant seeds, I could feel my body slumping over. My head hit the ground a few times. All I could think about was going to sleep. Just for a few minutes, that's all I need.

After we were done, we went over to the white barn to get med-checked. They were looking for signs of extreme fatigue and hypothermia. I was shaking badly. I was probably borderline hypothermic at that point but I was one of the last people to get checked and it gave me time to warm up. I had stopped shaking and we were in for another Joe special time. We were separated into three groups—physically strong, mentally strong, and the "weak". I was in the weak group. Now it was time for burpees. If Joe decided he picked wrong for you, he would move you to a new group. I stayed in the weak group. I felt like I was doing alright with the burpees but I wasn't going fast.

We now had to form teams from our group and start our next challenge. It was called the Denali challenge. We had to go up and down the mountain. To stay in the race, we had to do it 11 times. The first two times were with just our packs. I was teamed up with two girls who were a lot shorter than me. By the third trip, we had to carry a heavy slosh pipe filled with concrete. We were drained, but we couldn't give up.

At this point, it didn't matter how much it weighed, the three of us could not carry it. The height difference was a major factor. This was the point where it didn't seem possible to finish. The odds were stacked against us. While we were carrying it, it was accidentally dropped on my foot. The foot I didn't have shoelaces on. Why does that matter? I was sure it had broken my foot. I had to stop for a few minutes. A few racers stopped to check on me. I told them I would be fine in a few minutes. Luckily, Eric had shown up, he was running up and down the mountain for some reason.

I could have been hallucinating at this point because I swore he DNFd a day or two ago. He said he would help carry the pipe with us. I won't say no to that. Someone passing by us said that we should head back with the pipe and we have to carry wood now. When we got back, that's not what was supposed to happen and we were scolded accordingly.

I sat down. I remember getting called out for that. I had given it my all. I was drained. Now the medics had to look at me since the racers had told them someone was hurt. Please don't take off my shoe, is all I could think about. I didn't know if I'd get it back on. They took it off and checked my foot. Was I getting pulled? I couldn't believe this is how it ends. They said I was okay to go. I was amazed and very grateful.

Now, we had to carry a bucket full of firewood to the top. One girl was struggling. I grabbed her bucket and helped her as much as I could. After the next lap, we were on our own. I stayed with Amanda and someone else, we tried to stick together. We got a few more laps in before dawn. It was starting to get foggy. It was hard to see with the headlamps on. By morning, I had only done five laps. I stopped to rest before our next challenge. Amanda had gone for another lap.

At the end of the challenge, we had to line up and bear crawl to the fence. Now it was time for those penalty burpees. While we were doing the burpees, we were also being lectured. We had to memorize *The Man in the Arena* by Teddy Roosevelt. Some people were DNFd. You can pick the reason because I think it was made up, by them. While we were doing the burpees, we were also getting sprayed in the face with a garden hose.

With everyone that was left, we had to run over to the field across from Joe's house. This was it, the finale.

We were given the speech again about fear and reacting, with the skulls being shot with a shotgun. Amanda had attempted to run out and save one but was stopped. Later on, someone else had run out and she was declared the winner of the *Death Race*. With only seven skulls left, they were thrown in the pond, and anyone that wanted one, had to jump in and get it. With 18 people left, I had to try and get a skull for Kimball. I ran as fast as I could and jumped in.

I autographed the skull and sent it with Amanda to give to Kimball. The idea was I would give him this one. He would finish the *Death Race* and give me the one he earned.

I had finished. I earned the skull and finished all the bead challenges. I spelled out the word DEATH with them. I still have the bracelet that I made from it. The entire race had lasted 68 hours.

Beast of Burden 100 Summer

Ultra marathons are a different breed of race. Unless you've done one, it's hard to explain the draw to attempting them. It's one of the most physically and mentally taxing running events you can do. Other endurance events like the *GORUCK HTL*, *Death Race*, and similar events are not just straight running. There are heavy carries, teamwork, and shared pain. Unless you team up with someone, the odds are you are going to be by yourself for a while.

Pre-race most people knew me. They were familiar with my cold training and my ability to adapt. I do alright in the heat but the cold is where I shine. The forecast was calling for sunshine and temperatures in the 70s during the day and mid 50s overnight. There are a few issues with this course and I knew them all too well. There is very little shade on this course so you are baking in the sun for the bulk of the daylight hours. This is the most monotonous, flat course you can attempt. It literally feels like running on a treadmill for 100 miles. The tentative plan was to run 87 miles by myself and have Stefanie run the last leg back with me. Stefanie and Jess would be at the end aid stations helping me with whatever I needed.

For this race, Amy had to work, so I had to find other people to be my pit crew. Luckily Jess and Stefanie stepped up. Shawn stepped up and did a few miles with me as well.

First 25 miles

The goal was to stay fasted for the whole 25 mile loop, to run on water and *Heed,* an endurance drink mix . I was feeling great for the first seven miles, doing less than 10 minute miles. About 5−6 miles in, I got stung in the back of the head by a bee. Lucky, I'm not allergic but it was still pretty painful early in the race.

Jess was a little upset with me for going out too fast but I felt great. The pace wasn't straining me. Once I was out in the sun for a while, my pace started going down. Sub 10 minute miles turned into 11 minute miles. I was okay with that. I knew I would slow down from noon to four. I hit the Middleport aid station feeling great, just started to overheat a little bit, but cooled down for a few minutes before I headed back out. It was on my way to Middleport that I realized I had to start conserving water. I was running out before reaching the aid stations.

I put my headphones in after the Middleport station to change my mood. Going cheap on an MP3 player, I had to listen to the same few songs on repeat. Shuffle only kind of works. This was probably the lowest point in the race for me. After reaching Gasport I had to do something to turn this mood around. I made it 18 miles before I ate, I had a few pieces of watermelon. On the last few miles of this leg, I was trying to conserve water so I could make it back with some. I made it to the Day Road Bridge and luckily there was a girl sitting in the shade at the park. I asked her if she had water. She had *Powerade* and ice, Lifesaver!!! Ironically under the bridge, there was water and *Heed* just 50 feet further. I made it back in less then five hours.

25 mile Transition

Stefanie and Jess were waiting for me at the Lockport aid station. I was overheated and knew that if I didn't cool down, I was going to be in trouble for the next 25 miles. I was starting to feel dehydrated and hungry. I ate some ham, a brownie, and a snow cone. I refilled on water, had some anti-fatigue pills, salt tabs, and Advil.

25 to 50 mile

I started heading out and I got to the bridge. Of all the times I've done this race, I've never seen the bridge up. I learned you can go up the steps once the bridge is up or you can just wait—after running 26 miles, who wants to run up stairs? I had my headphones in for this part again. Still wish shuffle worked, but you really get to know the lyrics to a song if you hear it eight times in an hour. My pace was slowing down. I was walking more than I wanted to but I knew I was on a good pace. I wanted to make up time at night when it cooled down. One of the things about running after work, it was always dark. I had more training in the dark versus day time running.

50 mile Transition

I did change my outside socks but kept the *Injinis* on. Shawn was there and asked if I needed anything. I said back massage and as a great friend, he gave me a great massage. Stefanie helped me change my socks and gave me a good foot massage. Refuel, slight stretch, and head back out.

50 to 75 miles

Shawn showed and we suckered him into "running" to Orangeport with me. It was a nice change of pace. A little slower but talking with someone was keeping my mind off of the huge amount of miles I still had left. We were averaging a 17.5 minute mile, nothing super fast but steady. By the time we got to Orangeport (the *BTC* tent), Amy was waiting for us. Shawn left after some hugs and I was off with Amy to Middleport.

After a short bathroom break at the Gasport aid station, we were going at a fairly consistent pace, dropping down to a 15 minute pace. I had a slice of pizza and it just didn't sit right. I tried puking it back up and it just bogged me down. I stopped a few times and just bent over, hoping it would come back out. It finally settled by the time we got to Middleport. After getting to Middleport, I finally caught up to Billy. Fred was still 3–5 miles ahead of me at this point. Billy was in rough shape. Caffeine wasn't helping him and he tried sleeping but it didn't help.

Amy was going to pace me back to Lockport and Stefanie was going to pace me back to Middleport. That was the plan heading out. After about four miles, Amy was starting to crash. We weren't sure if it was sleep deprivation or hunger. So our plan had to change. Stefanie was going to meet us in Gasport and switch off with Amy.

When we got to Gasport, Billy was there and was in rough shape. Somebody came up with the plan for me and Stefanie to pace him back to Lockport. Hopefully, he would feel better once the sun came up. We stuck with the run then walk method. Running, I believe was a third on and off. We kept talking, keeping our minds off of the distance, and keeping ourselves awake. Stefanie was staying back a little bit, but finished a little after us.

75 mile Transition

I enjoyed another bathroom break, stretching, and eating. I had some grapes, another ice pop, watermelon, and coffee.

75 to 100 miles

We were still making good time. The goal was to finish. Slow and steady, we were still doing run and walk. It was a little after 6am when we left Lockport. We figured if we got to Middleport before 10am, then we could walk the rest of way and not have to rush. Not that we wanted to walk but it gave us a buffer if anything happened.

We caught up with Fred, who looked like he was having some issues. We passed him but he caught up to us and I asked if he wanted to stick with us. He thought we were on a time crunch but after some talking, we explained that we still had plenty of time. The goal was slow and steady. We had until 4pm to finish. So we kept each other talking. It made the miles go quicker. We made it to Middleport a little before 10am and we wanted to keep this aid station stop short and sweet. Refuel, stretch, bathroom visit, and head back out.

I decided to tape up my left foot because I was getting a hot spot by my big toe. We headed out with less than six hours to go 12.5 miles. Slow and steady, we were still doing run and walk but started doing every quarter mile now, enough to keep the legs fresh. About three miles in, I started to get shooting pains where the tape was. Was it the tape cutting into my foot or was the damage already done? Every step felt like I was getting stabbed in the foot. Keep pushing, don't think about the pain. I made it this far, no time to quit now. Just keep breathing and focus on finishing. I still had to get back, might as well get the buckle.

We stopped for a few minutes at the Gasport station. I had a peanut butter and jelly sandwich, a couple salt tabs, and some water. Fred was starting to fall behind a little more and we decided it would basically be a walk to get back now. Around six miles left, the plan was to see how we felt at mile four, and mile three, and try to break up the last stretch. We were so close and didn't want to do anything stupid. We stopped after the bridge to cross over the canal, made it just before it went up. We had two more people join our merry group, Justin and Raina.

We finished as a big group. I thought that was pretty cool. At the finish line, I couldn't get my shoes off fast enough. I told Amy to have buckets of ice ready for my feet. It was a little tough to eat afterward. I got a chicken sandwich and a chocolate milkshake for my post race meal. The ice was soothing and cut down some of the swelling. I took a shower while I waited for my food. I only had some minor chaffing, nothing like the *Philly HTL*. My feet were sore but I've definitely been worse. No blisters, no major injuries—just soreness.

North American OCR Championship

Qualifying for *Nor-Am Age-Group* or *OCR Worlds* was difficult. There were so many different ways to do it but essentially you have to be in the top percentage of an *OCR* race. I had qualified in 2017 for *Journeymen*, 2018 for *Age Group at Shale Hill.* I got the e-mail in May. This had been one of my goals for this year. It turns out running one lap of *Shale Hill* was deemed sufficient for *Age-Group.* The pressure was off for the rest of my races. I was able to enjoy the rest of the races I had that year.

The 3k

Now the pressure was on. I had to show that I was better than last year at *OCR Worlds.* I made it a lot farther without losing my band but still lost it on a rig. I tried until my hands were bloody and then finally lost my band. Had I known that my foot didn't hit the ground, it would have counted. I thought my foot touched the ground but it had only hit the hay. I went through the rest of the course fairly bitter, but I shook it off after a mile. The pain hurt more than the failure now. I finished missing only a few obstacles. It took me awhile to realize that I had greatly improved.

Volunteering the 15k

The 3k was a bust for me. I wanted to keep my band so bad and tore up my hands in the process. I had my hands taped up and we were all going to volunteer on the course for the 15k. Amy and Stefanie were going to be at skull valley. I was going to be at skitch. It was a great experience cheering on runners. Then it sucked because I did have to cut bands off of the runners that couldn't complete the obstacle. I only had to do a couple but it was painful to watch them struggle for so long and finally give up. The obstacle was difficult since you had to use hooks to get across the bar. A lot of people hurt their hands when they clanked together. The hooks were removed from the team course on Sunday.

Running Team

For some reason, I was picked to run technical. Amy was going to do speed. Stefanie was going to run the strength leg of the race. The night before, Dragon's Back was switched from not being in the race to being added to the speed leg. It's not a hard obstacle but more of a mental mind game. You have to jump from platform to platform to finish the obstacle. The distance gets wider as you reach each platform. We would find out when Amy finished that she was trying to keep her band but was having a hard time working up to jumping. She finally lost her band after multiple attempts.

We were in dead last. Not that it mattered. We were just trying to have fun with it at this point. Stefanie would take over next and go through the Strength leg. and she would struggle at the same obstacle that I failed at *Worlds*, le Gaffe. She would lose her band there but continue on with her portion. Now it was my time to shine. I didn't care at that point. I had tried so hard on the 3k and I lost my band. I was going to have fun now. I was doing really good and playing on the obstacles. I finished obstacles that I had always had a hard time with. I was having a great time.

I met Marissa on a rope swing obstacle. I gave her a few words of encouragement since we were now one of the last teams on the course. We posed for pictures since the camera person was sitting there. Why not? There were only a few obstacles left so why not play around on them. We finished it pretty close to each other. She remembered me from volunteering Saturday. It was definitely more fun to run without thinking about being competitive. I did better and made a new friend out there.

6

2021

With 2020 being a wash, it was nice because it gave me time to recover. I had been dealing with a foot issue nagging me since the *GORUCK Cincinnati Star Course*. Going to doctors had not solved my issue, and it was finally visiting a chiropractor that I was able to walk without pain. I had done my first half *Ironman* distance triathlon called *Cassadagaman*. For me, it was nice since there was no time limit. I had big plans going into 2021, I wanted to qualify for *Western States 100*, and the goal was to do as many 100 milers as I could fit into my schedule. I had *Eastern States 100*, *Mighty Mosquito*, *Pistol Ultra* virtual, and the *Keys 100* on my list. *Badwater 135* was in my sights, and finishing the *Keys 100* would give me a slight advantage when sending in my application. I wasn't planning on doing as many OCR's this year and was trying to focus on long distances. I had also planned on finishing the PA Triple Crown this year and had signed up for the 3 races needed, *Hyner*, *World's End*, and *Eastern States*. I had finished *Hyner*, DNF'd *World's End*, and well *Eastern States*...that was a bust. This would be the year I realize it's not how you start, but how you come back from adversity.

Keys 100

Sometimes you make a plan for a race and sometimes it works out. This would not be the race. It was supposed to be me and Amy but silly me; I thought it would be a great idea to bring the kids. We stayed in Florida City before the race and planned to go back there after the race. The problem was that this race was a point to point, so if we left the kids at the hotel, at the farthest point, we would be over a hundred miles away. Change of plans— I would start the race in the morning and Amy would take the kids and get a hotel around the halfway point. There is only one road in and out of Key Largo. We didn't consider traffic as a problem.

Mile 1–20

I had a late start since I signed up after all the early corral times were gone. No biggie, I had 32 hours from the time I started. That would give me until 3:20pm Sunday to finish. I would start with a hydration bladder, sunglasses, and a hat. I wouldn't see Amy until close to mile 17. Traffic was bad getting back to me. I was on my own for a lot longer than I had hoped. I stopped at a gas station to get some water and used the bathroom. Amy finally found me and I refueled. This would be the theme of the race, pushing farther than I wanted without refueling.

Mile 21–40

This was going to be the hardest part of the race. If I could maintain a brisk pace and not overheat, I should be able to speed up later in the afternoon. Unfortunately, the heat was brutal. I wasn't used to running in the exposed sun with no shade in sight. Keep pushing forward is all I could think about. I was on point with hydration and was moving forward. The pace was slower than I was hoping for but it was in the right direction. I remember reaching the medical checkpoint. They walked with me, made sure I had a crew, and checked that I was okay to keep going. Did I not look okay? Was this something they did with everyone? I didn't ask and just kept going. I told them I was going to run once the sun went down. I'm sure they laughed at that.

Miles 41–60

Almost to the halfway point, changing socks, underwear, and shoes was crucial to keeping me from falling apart. I would keep pushing along at a steady pace, slightly faster than I was going earlier. The hotel we had was closer to the end of Marathon and would be a stopping point to regear, take a quick shower, and eat. The hardest part of the race was coming up, the seven mile bridge. I would be on my own until I reached the other side. After I left the hotel, it started to downpour which sounds bad, but it felt great. I was soaked and heading into the longest bridge of the course. It only rained for 10–20 minutes. The wind kicked up after. I was out in the open. The wind was to my back and it gave me a nice boost. I ran the bulk of the bridge. It was a little scary running into traffic with no sidewalks. I kept wondering if I was on the right side of the bridge, as it looked like there was a walkway on the other side of the road. I decided to stay on this side and it paid off. The checkpoint and timing mat were on my side. Another quick stop for refuel and I was off again.

Miles 61–80

This would be the overnight part of the race, pushing me into early morning before I reached the lower Keys. I was doing a run then walk, keeping a brisk pace. Everything was going well for the most part. I was walking with someone for a little bit. Then I started to go at a faster pace and I was gone.

Miles 80 to Finish

My body was spent. The miles and heat had taken a toll but I wasn't done yet. I kept looking at the map on my phone and willing myself to get to the next island. One Island at a time, that's all I can do. I was at a terrible pace and running was questionable at best. I was trying to stay focused. My logic was completely flawed, quite possibly delusional at that point. I really thought I'd made the Sugarloaf Key disappear. When I reached it, I was shocked it was there. It's okay. After this, there is just one more Key before Key West, easy enough.

Sometimes I feel like I should read the map of the race but where's the fun in that? When I finally reached Key West, I felt like I had two miles left. The worst part was that Amy didn't help me realize I had more. The finish line was right around the bend. Okay, so let's have Alexis run the last mile with me. I had just enough water left to go a mile. Yet again, I should have looked at the map correctly. It was 2.4 miles to the finish line. How was I that far off? I definitely wasn't going to tell Alexis that, just a little bit farther.

We reached a point where I could jump in the water real quick and cool off. As I was walking out of the water someone offered us two bottles of water. It could have been an angel, I'm not sure. We finally reached the last half mile and I could see the end. We ran the last 300 feet. I finished at that point. It was my hardest 100 miler. I got my buckle and jumped into the ocean (I really just collapsed). I had no strength left to get up and the waves kept knocking me over. My legs were jelly. I was trying to stretch in the water.

Before we headed back, the kids wanted lunch and to go shopping. I remember going to a Mexican restaurant, ordering food, and when I took a sip of water, I passed out. They just let me sleep as they ate. I hobbled to the back of the truck and slept on the air mattress. We must have teleported to Florida City because I don't remember any part of the trip. Our room was on the second floor, there was no elevator. No elevator, that's just evil. I made it to the room and slept some more. I would finish the race in 29 hours 39 minutes. I feel like I made a lot of mistakes in this race, some poor planning and not training enough for the race. The heat was the biggest factor. I know I could've done better if I had planned my crew stops better. Gear was mostly on point and changing socks kept my feet happy. There were no major issues afterwards, just the heat and being tired.

Leadville Marathon

The Drive out To Colorado

Originally, it was going to be a family trip but the kids still had school. We drove out the day before to get acclimated. Once we reached Denver, we found a Pizza Hut, never the best idea before a race.

After packet pickup, we walked around Leadville and visited each store. A superstition says that getting race gear before you finish a race is a bad idea. I got a sweater. People don't realize that an XL does not fit taller people and I'm kind of chunky. We tried finding a good restaurant to eat at but there wasn't anything I would eat. We stopped at a local grocery store. I got ham, a salad, peppers, and chocolate milk. I tried doing a short run the night before and ran up and down the stairs of our hotel to get my heart rate up. I wasn't feeling great. I knew I wasn't going all out on this race. I just wanted to finish within the eight hour time limit. That's plenty of time for a marathon, well, a normal marathon. I decided against using trekking poles and told Amy to use them instead.

The first 14 miles

I was worried about how I would feel with the difference in elevation but the rush of adrenaline made me feel great. I was firing on all cylinders. Those first few miles, my heart rate was staying in zone three, but I was flying. I walked up steep hills but for the majority of the time I was running. I felt like a gazelle on the down hills. This was turning out to be one of my best trail runs. I wasn't pushing hard, this felt like a good tempo run.

When I hit the aid station before Mosquito Pass, I stopped to refill my water bottle. I also grabbed a quick snack, just a few cookies to hold me over. The terrain changed to a rocky stream, just rocky enough that I didn't trust running.

The climb to Mosquito Pass

It wasn't far to the next aid station. It was at the top of Mosquito Pass. This was the steepest climb in the race and the highest elevation I had ever been at during a race. I had to walk up the incline. I didn't trust my footing with the rocks. The higher up I went, the more snow I saw. My heart rate was climbing with every step. It was getting harder to breathe. It was almost like I was gasping for breath. Focus, I needed to get my heart rate down and stop panicking. I got this, one foot in front of the other.

The wind was picking up now since I was out in the open. It was getting rough. I started to panic. My heart was beating out of my chest. Is it from the altitude or because I lacked focus? I just had to get to the top and regroup. I was almost crawling up the mountain and racers were starting to pass me. It's okay, just keep moving forward. It's like the *Death March* at Killington. I did that, why can't I do this? People were coming down, cheering us on as we were still climbing up. Almost there, they said. I couldn't talk, so I just smiled and nodded. Just a little bit more. The wind is really picking up. It's getting harder to breathe. Just focus on getting to the next aid station.

Finally, I made it. The wind was brutal, making it hard to breathe. I grabbed a gel pack, refilled my water, ate a salt tab, and got off the mountain as fast as possible. I thought being at the aid station would give me a break from the wind, but no. I start heading down, with a slow run to start. The rocks are difficult to run on so I start walking down. That's when it happened. I tripped on a rock and started to fall. I caught myself before I fell on my face.

My calf cramped up. It felt like a big Charlie horse. I stopped to stretch it out and grabbed a rock to rub my calf. A few runners stopped to offer me a salt tab but I had just had one so I thought I was going to be okay. Just get down the mountain. After hobbling down a half mile, I ran into Amy going up the mountain. She didn't have the trekking poles which I was praying she had. She gave me two ibuprofens. I told her what happened. I figured I would walk it off by the next aid station. If I was in more pain, then I would quit. I could still shuffle run and I still had plenty of time to finish.

I got to the aid station. I wasn't in pain. It was more discomfort than anything. It felt like if I kept moving that I wasn't doing any damage. If something was wrong, stopping now wasn't going to change it. Stretching wasn't helping. I figured I'd get to the next aid station and reassess. I've walked in more pain than this. Amy said she left the trekking poles at that next aid station. Now I just had to remember to grab them. I was going with a shuffle run then walk to keep myself moving forward. Just get to the aid station. That's all I could focus on.

I was just a few hundred feet from the finish line, finally this was over. Everyone was cheering as I started to run to the finish. Then it happened. My legs just stopped working. I froze in pain. I couldn't move. Time froze. The finish line was there ten feet in front of me. It felt like miles.

The ER in Leadville and heading to Denver

The medics grabbed me after I finished and sat me down in a chair. I couldn't move my right leg and it had swollen badly. It felt like my entire calf was as hard as a rock. My first instinct was to find Amy and go back to the hotel room and soak in the tub. Maybe that would help. The medics got their boss. He told me I had to go to the ER and asked if I had a ride. I thought Amy would have caught up to me at this point. I waited for her to pass me for miles but I hadn't seen her. I didn't know how close to the cutoff I was. She had DNFd awhile back helping another runner. I was more in shock than in pain. The only thing I could think about was how long I would be out for. Could I still do *Eastern States*? I had many races still to do. I couldn't be out too long. This would just be a hiccup in the plan.

Amy finally found me and the medics helped me into our truck. We would head over to the ER in Leadville. Instead of using the GPS, we went the wrong way and drove around town for a little bit. The nurses got me a wheelchair. I had to fill out paperwork. Meanwhile Amy was parking the car. I just felt like crap. I was getting dizzy and my vision was starting to go dark. I kept telling them I didn't feel good. Then everything went black. They didn't have a room for me so I just sat in the hallway.

I finally saw a doctor and got a bed. The doctor thought I had compartment syndrome and he couldn't treat it there. We would have to go to Denver. They could send me in an ambulance or we could drive. I was afraid of the insurance bill and the lack of food for the two hour drive. I hadn't eaten or drunk anything since I finished the race. Now we were going on three hours with nothing more than water. The pain hadn't set in yet. We left the hospital. I was starving so we went to Starbucks because I also needed caffeine.

The doctor offered me pain medicine for the ride which I should have taken because after 20 minutes of driving, the pain finally hit. I couldn't get comfortable in the truck. I was cramping up, every bump in the road was agonizing. I just wanted out of the truck. I knew stopping would just make this longer. They told us this was a very time-sensitive injury and I could die.

Denver

Amy dropped me off at the ER so she could park. I was still in a lot of pain but at least I could stretch out now. After going through the check in, they decided to send me to the ICU. To this day, I still don't know what they said to me that first night. What I remember is that there was a chance I could die, that my kidneys and heart were having problems. I was experiencing Rhabdomyolysis. My kidneys couldn't keep up. There was a faint pulse in my foot. They were worried that they would either have to cut my leg open to relieve the pressure on my veins and arteries or cut my leg off at the knee. If my foot had lost blood, there would be no saving it. I had to be prepped for surgery. No food or water was allowed because I could go at any time. They had to check my foot for a pulse every 45 minutes to ensure I still had blood flow.

The shock of the situation was starting to sink in. When something traumatizing is happening to you, there are a few ways you can deal with it. I like to add humor. The more serious the situation, the more I joke around. They were using an ultrasound to check my foot. The only time I've seen an ultrasound used was for pregnancy. Please don't tell me that my foot is pregnant, I don't know if I can handle a third foot. For the phone calls I had to make, I would play them off like this was an extended vacation. Everything was going to be fine. That's what I told myself.

I was allowed to leave on Tuesday, and I got to keep my leg intact. The swelling really didn't go down but it wasn't worse. My kidney levels were in the safe zone finally. We had a long drive back. It was 23 hours back without stopping. Before we left Denver, we were going to stop at a grocery store and stock up on food and drinks for the ride. There was a card store next to the grocery store. I had to go in. I was still in my hospital gear and had flip flops on. I love checking out game stores. You never know what collectibles you might find. I found a Nintendo 64 on this trip so at least I had that to play since I couldn't do anything else.

Amy did most of the driving back. I did some and was glad we didn't have the manual Jeep anymore. The doctor didn't say I couldn't drive but it was hard to hit the petals so I only drove the highway with very little traffic.

Buffalo ER

We got back Wednesday evening. It was a struggle getting in and out of the truck let alone into the house. I could move around a little bit and the doctor didn't say anything about staying in bed. I could barely do anything with my leg down. The pain was so bad; I spent the rest of the night in bed. Once Thursday hit, I couldn't get out of bed without being in excruciating pain. How badly do I have to use the bathroom? Even lying down hurt. I just couldn't get comfortable while lying down. Something wasn't right, I just didn't know what.

I ended back in the ER in Buffalo after going to the doctor's Friday morning. I would find out while I was there that I was having heart issues. I had to go for every test they could think of to see what was going on. They also had to check my leg to see if anything else was wrong and why I was in so much pain. I found out later that I had torn my calf, my meniscus, and may have more tears but they couldn't see them in the images. I left the hospital in a boot that I couldn't even put my foot on the ground. At least I had my walker to assist me. I had been told by every doctor there that I was done running. That was depressing. I spiraled into self wallowing and retreated from the world.

GORUCK World Championship

GORUCK had come up with a new idea for a race, based on the *GORUCK* Star course. Anyone who had completed a Star course of 26 miles or more was qualified for this new event. There would be big cash prizes versus the gift codes and free event codes offered for the other Star courses. The bonus was that they came up with a new ruck specifically designed for this race, the Speed Rucker. If you signed up for the first ever *GORUCK World Championship* in Washington DC, you got the Speed Rucker included. Sign me up.

This would be the first time they offered teams or individuals.

In most Star courses, you had to start with at least two people on your team. You could finish as an individual but were not able to win any prizes. I learned this at Columbus when I finished by myself. Rob had offered the idea for us to do it as a team. At the time, it sounded like a good idea. But this was in 2019 and Covid 19 would delay the championship until November 2021. That worked to my advantage at the time since I really wasn't able to ruck long distances. Unfortunately, I would get hurt again and this would be way worse.

I had only done a half marathon distance race, the *EVL half* with a 30lb ruck to see if I had a chance in DC. The half would be my first ruck since getting hurt in June. Could my body handle it? I had just finished *Cassadagaman* triathlon a few weeks ago and was feeling alright. *Cassadagaman* had a half marathon but there wasn't a time limit, so if it took me all day, it wasn't a problem. I did it and I wasn't last but I was in rough shape after. Usually, I come up with bad ideas, was this one of them? Amy was going to be out there as well, so I had her to fall back on for support. I had done the course a few times so I knew what to expect. I finished the half in 2 hours 39 minutes and 30 seconds which wasn't my worst, more impressive was that I had a 30lb ruck on.

DC was looking possible. I just couldn't overdo training and had to figure out a working plan. This is where the idea of the book can from. How could I go from doing a half marathon to an ultra in only a few weeks?

In the back of my mind, I had doubts about whether I could ever do an ultra again. Would my heart give out? Was I ready to come back? The doctor never told me what was wrong with my heart and that bothered me. I have high blood pressure but I've had high blood pressure for years. There was that fear that this would either end up in a DNF or I was going to end up back in the hospital. But how would I know if I didn't try?

So you have those Facebook friends that you've never met in real life and you try to follow their journey. One guy, Robert, had a similar story to how I started out running and getting into shape. I had given him a code for a *GORUCK* event. I also gave him an entry into *Green Beret Operation OCALA* in the hopes that he would use that in some way to change his luck. I remember feeling like the world was against me. I wish I could have done more but I thought that was a good start. That would come up later in the story.

Okay, Amy booked the hotel right next to the start point. It was the closest I had ever been to the start of a race. We drove down that day and got into DC around 4:30pm. The event started at 9pm, but I had to be there for check-in at 8pm. I didn't have a strategy going into this like I normally do. I literally forgot half my stuff for check-in. I had no sweater, no food, and little water. I did have my map, my 30lb plate, and my clipboard with paper.

What I didn't know was that this wasn't going to be a normal *Star* course. There wasn't plotting a course with multiple points. It was a point to point and they would tell you the coordinates for each point one at a time. Okay, that makes it a little easier for me. I don't have to worry about plotting a terrible course or forgetting a point again. But this also made it easier for someone to just run to the points. Any advantage someone had with plotting a course was out the window.

We would go out in three waves, two would be the individuals, and the last one would be teams. I would be in the second group with Robert. I finally met him and wished him luck. I said I would run with him but I doubted that I could keep up with anyone. I had very low expectations for this race. Finishing was my main objective but also not getting hurt. The turnout was less than I expected but I think there were over a hundred people there. I was trying to keep a low profile. I didn't think I belonged there. I just wanted to focus on my race and hopefully hobble through it.

Trail and road running are not the same. If you have knee issues on the impact of concrete or road, trail running is more forgiving. Running with a ruck is discouraged as it could affect your gait and cause more damage to your knees. I had not trained with a ruck as much as I wanted to or should have.

We were set to go. We each got a slip of paper that would lead us to the first waypoint. Usually, a waypoint is a location like a city hall or a museum. Instead, this was latitude and longitude points. Okay, now I have to think about this for a second. How do you navigate that way? I put it into *Google Maps*, bam, now I have an idea of where I'm going. I show the Cadre the waypoint and he nodded his head, I'm good to go. I take off running and there are two people ahead of me going at a brisk pace. I can do that pace and it's not a struggle.

I forgot to take *Google Maps* off of car mode and put it into walking mode. I realized it after about a mile and a half. Okay, that problem is solved. The guys I'm following are starting to go a little faster, they also had their phones in driving mode. They missed a pedestrian walkway that shaved a little bit off. Now I'm the lead, but not for long. They passed me after a few minutes. My running speed was slowing down. I was still running but closer to an eleven minute mile.

I never started my watch. Did it matter? Did I care? Nope. This was going to be fun, I couldn't take it seriously. I was playing *Pokemon GO* as we were doing this event. I brought headphones thinking I was going to be alone for the bulk of the race but I never turned them on. About 4–5 miles in, I caught up to someone. I could see he was having a bad time and dropped his bag on the ground. As I passed him, I said good job. I was trying to be encouraging and I've yet to come up with something better to say. I'm pretty sure he told me to F off, which took me by surprise, but I kept going. What else could I do? There was very little I could do to help someone else, let alone myself for this race.

I was coming to a more lit-up area. I would have to go over a bridge to get across traffic. The guy was a little behind me and said there was a shortcut. I said okay. I didn't know where to look so I just stayed on track. We eventually caught up to each other and he apologized for swearing at me. I didn't mind that he swore at me, everyone has that moment when you break down. I just wasn't expecting it that early in the race. We stuck together for a while. I was curious about what had happened. He was upset that the race wasn't going as expected.

It wasn't land navigation. If you weren't running, you weren't going to win. He had hoped to do a lot better and I totally understood. I told him my goal was to finish. I told him about my injury and that I wasn't going to push too hard. He wanted to drop. I said at least get to the first waypoint and reassess. Little did I know that I would need his help to finish.

I don't want to get too far ahead but it's funny how things work out. We would both help each other finish this event. Ironically, we have the same name, but he would spell it Thom. He knew DC better than I did. I had no idea where the major landmarks were or what part of town we were in. You don't really need to know that but it probably helps.

There are a few grips I have about this event. They've

been addressed since but at the time it provided either a huge advantage or a disadvantage to the event. That is outside help. Thom and I both had outside help but it wasn't a rule. It should have been. It would be a lot easier to resupply with a crew than carrying everything you need for the entire event. End of rant.

Thom was an interesting person. He had many stories of the *Star* courses he did but he wasn't a fan of the regular *GORUCK* events, which is totally understandable. It's not everyone's cup of tea. He had done *Tokyo* and *Normandy*, which I would love to do someday. We kept talking and it made the time pass. At each waypoint, we would get another piece of paper and head off. We stuck together. He probably could have left me after a few hours but he stayed. Eventually, we added people into our group but they were moving too fast for us to keep pace.

By our fourth waypoint, we were heading back to the start line. We knew we weren't done but this kept us close together. The waypoints were designed to only be a few miles from the start point. Which was nice for our pit crews, they didn't have to drive 20 miles out of the way.

By the time we reached the last waypoint, we couldn't find the *GORUCK* tent. It wasn't a huge park but it wasn't small. We decided to split up after walking around the park. I said it had to be somewhere close to the road and we should walk the perimeter of the park. Thom would find it first but it was a car, not a tent.

That would have been important to know when they sent us out. We spent at least a half hour looking through that park. We got to the last waypoint and it was the start point again. Getting there should give us around 50 miles. I finished at 16 hours, 24 minutes, and 40 seconds, which would be one of my fastest 50 mile *Star* course times. We never stopped too long for anything.

Bathroom breaks were probably the longest. It was more trying to find somewhere open that would let us use their restroom.

7

2022

2022

I still hadn't learned to take things easy and I was looking for big events to do. I wasn't sure how good of a runner I could still be, but I knew I could still ruck. I was asked to do a Green Beret event last year, but the injury sidelined me. There was another event in Florida, and it was being sold as one of the hardest Green Beret events. Sign me up. I still had my deferral for Operation Stirling and this would be a good test. I had to go back to the Keys and try and redeem myself for the trainwreck of a race that was. I finished but I knew I could do better with more planning. This year I would be signing up for races as I went through the year. I didn't want to commit if I got hurt again. I went back to doing OCR's and did *Bonefrog, Black Swamp Dash* so far. Nothing beats volunteering and then running. I was still recognized on the course, and it was nice seeing old friends that I had lost touch with. Sometimes it's nice to get away from the drama of the groups but you lose connections with the people that push you to do great things.

Operation OCALA

I wasn't prepared enough for this event but I was going to grind it out, 65 miles, no big deal. Twenty-five pound ruck, easy enough, especially since it didn't have to be dead weight. I had the gear list: water, food, medical kit, two battery packs, emergency sleeping bag (bivy), emergency blanket, $30, salt tabs, dry bag, headphones, compass, pocket knife, extra pair of socks, headlamp, batteries, pain medicine, and caffeine pills.

The trail was well marked in some areas but then there were points where it wasn't marked for a mile or more. I was told to use the *All Trails* app for navigation, but after a mile, I gave up on it. I used *Life360*, so that Amy could keep an eye on me. It came in handy because she could see when I was coming into the checkpoints and if I got off course, which happened a few times. This was probably the easiest trail run I've ever done in terms of ground and elevation. There was just enough elevation to be annoying and switch up the muscle groups. There were roots, branches, and trees but nothing like running in Pennsylvania or New York where a misstep means broken bones or a face plant. The sand was different, and sucked to walk or run in.

Nutrition

I love *Sour Patch Kids*, it's my go-to for ultra events. I brought two little bags, nothing huge. I also brought in my ruck: licorice, beef jerky, and my minimum of two candy bars. I had my three liter hydration bladder, one liter water bottle, one Powerade (sugar free) and one extra water bottle. I ate a few cookies, Reese's cups, and peanut butter sandwiches at the checkpoints.

Running gear

I wore Inov-8 g-fly trail shoes, two pairs of socks, pants, my *SISU Iron* finisher shirt, sunglasses, and a hat. I did not change gear or socks. I didn't take any kind of special care. I should have, but I didn't. Also, don't try a new pair of underwear for an ultra race.

Miles 1–15 (checkpoint 1) When we took off at 9am, everyone seemed to be walking at a brisk pace. One guy started to shuffle run. I caught up with him and talked for a few minutes before I started to run. I figured I would run for as long as I could then switch to run then walk. After bringing out a good lead on everyone, I wasn't paying attention to the orange markings and just happened to see the markings on the trees. I had my sunglasses on in the shade. I happened to take them off and I was on the white trail. I had gone off course and had to back track. Fair enough, that was on me.

After getting back on course, a guy with trekking poles passed me. He didn't seem to want to talk. I tried keeping up with him or to at least keep him in sight. It worked for a little bit but then he was gone. I got lost again near the first lake but quickly got back on course. Then the course split, east and west. Follow the orange trail— but they're both orange! I don't remember anyone saying anything about this. They have to merge again, I thought. But given the choice go east, I went east. Amy called me telling me after I should have gone east (sic). I made it to the first checkpoint in first place. Where did the other guy go? Not the right way.

Miles 16–30 (checkpoint 2) It was going to get hot. I knew it was going to be in the 70s and I was going to have to slow down or overheat. I grabbed my trekking poles for this leg of the course. I figured it would save my legs for later. Things were going well. It was warm and I was keeping a decent pace without running. I made it to Hopkins Prairie and finally, someone was behind me. I wasn't going to speed up, just keep running my race. It was probably around mile twenty-five when they both caught up to me. We started talking and stayed together for a few miles.

France took off. Ken and I were still walking together at a brisk pace. We made it to the campground and caught up to France again. We checked *All Trails* to make sure we didn't miss the checkpoint. It was still a mile or two farther. She took off again. At the checkpoint, I waited for Amy and Ken took off. A few other guys caught up to me and we talked briefly. I headed back out without the trekking poles. I had the headlamp on my head, I left my sunglasses and hat with Amy.

Miles 31–45 (checkpoint 3)

Ok, so they were ahead of me, I was still in third. Third is pretty good, nothing wrong with that. My goal was just to finish. The only problem is that I'm not pushing and I know that I'm still fresh. They were not, they were starting to hurt. The sun was going down and I got my second wind. It took me awhile but I caught up to France, which shocked me. I thought I would catch Ken first. I asked her if she was okay or needed anything, she said she was good, so I started running again. I kept going. I stopped seeing orange markings, so I called Amy to make sure I was still on the right trail. I was and she told me I could cut off a chunk if I went straight through the woods. Every ounce of my being thought that was a terrible idea. While I was on the phone, I could hear yelling.

It was Ken and he was lost in the woods. I yelled to him so he could find the trail again. He found me and we stuck together as it was starting to get dark. We hit a water crossing and lost the trail. I crossed looking for the trail, found it and as we started again, France caught us. We decided to stick together as it would be our best bet to finish. Unfortunately it didn't stay that way. Ken was starting to slow down and his feet were starting to hurt badly. I started going faster and assumed they would stick together. I made it to the checkpoint a little while later. I didn't stop too long. I asked Amy for new batteries since I didn't want to look in my ruck for them. She gave me a different headlamp. I had a peanut butter sandwich and took off.

Miles 46–60 (checkpoint 4) I was still feeling good. After about a mile, my headlamp started flashing red. Great, dead batteries. I wasn't going back and I was too lazy to get the batteries out. I wanted to push. I didn't want to stop. I didn't know if France was going for first. It pushed me to keep going at a brisker pace. I would've been okay just walking the rest. Stupid pride, keep pushing. Luckily the moon was out and I could see really well in the dark. I would just flick my light on for a few seconds to make sure I was still on the trail.

Miles 60–66(finish) I came into the checkpoint at around fifty-eight miles, just a few miles to go. As I took off, I punched in the pizza place to see how far I had to go. It said I had nine miles to—um that didn't seem right. It's probably because I'm on the trail. Just keep going. I hit the road and *Google Maps* said the trail head was a quarter mile up the road. Okay, perfect, I was walking and looking, nothing. Okay, maybe it's a little further. Nothing—I call Amy and ask if I'm going the right way. She said I passed the trail. Okay, I go back, still don't see it.

Let's walk a little bit and see if I can find it. After about fifty feet, I found a trail, perfect. Just keep pushing. I'm still running and walking. I can't let her catch me. I have to make her earn it. After hitting the end of the trail, I have about 2.5 miles of road to run, the only problem, it's a sand road. My legs were killing me.

Running in sand is brutal sixty miles into an event. I got to a real road and I have just a little over a mile left. I learned at the end, that I went the wrong way and came in from the wrong direction. I finished with 66.27 miles in 18 hours and 27 minutes.

Skydive 100

I had been going back and forth on whether I should do this race and brought some stuff down for racing just in case. Did I bring everything I needed for a 100 miler? Nope. We flew down Thursday and the race was Saturday. Should I do the 100 miler, 100k, or anything shorter? Should I skydive, or just save myself the extra money? I definitely wasn't feeling 100%, and the flight down messed with my sinuses. Our car rental was a bust. That's why you should always check reviews on hotels and car rental places. Okay, so no car. We didn't book a hotel for Thursday night. The plan was to stay in Fort Lauderdale the first night and head up to the hotel we booked near the venue Friday afternoon. We used an *Uber* for the first time to get to our hotel. This would be the first time we used *Door Dash* as well to get drinks and sinus medicine for me. I was feeling stuffy Friday morning but I had to decide what I was doing. I went for the buckle. Anything less wouldn't be as challenging. If I wanted to accomplish big things, I'd have to push for them. Just be smart about it. It's a looped course, so if anything happened, I wouldn't get stranded on the course. Thirty-two hours on a flat course should give me plenty of time without pushing too hard.

The skydive

If you're going to do a sky dive ultra, you have to skydive, otherwise, what's the point? The only problem was I was added so late, that I was one of the last people to jump for the 100 miler. Had I not checked with the desk, I wouldn't have jumped. Luckily they added me to the third flight. I would be jumping with Amy. Kaine was going to be my tandem jumper. He was a seasoned instructor so I was in good hands. It was about then that I found out that the skydive cuts into your total time. Okay, I should still have about thirty-one hours to finish. I had done a sky dive before, but if you know me, you know I hate planes, falling, and heights. It's about going against your fears and pushing yourself. This time we would be going up to 15,000 feet and jumping. I feel like that was pretty high up and it was chilly in the morning. The jump went good but I hate the feeling of free-falling and being unable to breathe. We landed and I couldn't hear, I remember Kaine saying something about going inside for something. I was now two hours behind. I grabbed my bib and my timing bracelet and start running.

Running gear

So I started the race with pants and my *SISU* shirt. I wore my *Brooks* road shoes, not knowing what the course was like. I would later change into shorts and put on my hat. I only had a water bottle since I didn't bring anything to hold my stuff. Later after Amy was done, I would get the running belt. I also had trekking poles for later in the race.

First lap.

I came out at a decent pace. There would be no way to gauge how I was doing compared to everyone else. I had to focus on my race and not do anything crazy. The goal was to finish and not get hurt. I was getting a feel for what I was getting into. Fourteen laps were going to be tough. The wind was picking up. It was going to be rough running into the wind for the first three miles. After the first lap, I switched to shorts and refilled my bottle then headed back out.

Second lap

The sun was out and I knew heat could be a factor. I kept a decent pace and watched for overheating. I slowed down a little bit but nothing drastic. I was averaging a twelve minute pace. Just keep drinking and moving forward.

3rd lap

I caught up to Amy by the end of the second lap. She was getting stuff out of the truck and saw me coming. I refilled my bottle, grabbed some jerky, a few *Sour Patch Kids* and headed back out. Things were still going alright. I was keeping a decent pace and still running.

4th lap

Amy was still running so I didn't have a crew yet. I was okay. I still didn't have anything to hold my bottle or any food. On this lap, I changed my socks for something with more cushion. It wasn't hot out anymore and I wasn't worried about overheating. The pacing was still going good, I was still running.

5th lap

I was still keeping a steady pace and it had started to cool down. I was doing a run/walk and was feeling good. Nothing really extraordinary happened on this lap.

6th lap

On this lap, I caught up to someone who was going my pace. His name was Joel. We started walking together. One of the best things about doing these races is you definitely meet some interesting people. Joel was a badass guy who's done multiple 100 milers. He was even at the *Keys 100* when I did it. He was worried about the cold coming at night. That's his downfall on these kinds of races. He started running once we were past the aid station. I tried to keep up. After a mile, he was starting to put distance between us and I had to pee.

By the time I hit the inside of the sugar canes looking into the airport side, it was time to stop and pee. Joel was out of eyesight by the time I started running again. I would come into the aid station, grab some salt tabs, and switch my sunglasses for a headlamp. The one girl we were talking to before the race, Alicia, told me that Amy had left for the hotel. I was a little irked because I was hoping to grab the headlamp and food for this lap. She went and got a headlamp for me and took my sunglasses. I started off and then Amy yelled to get my attention. I wasn't even looking for her. Bam, I got my stuff. I was off before sunset.

7th lap

Fifty miles in, what am I doing? I still have 50 miles to go. It seems overwhelming. This was the point at which I was definitely questioning why I was doing this. Don't think about it, just keep moving. I asked Amy to get me new insoles for my shoes. I knew the ones I had wouldn't last me the rest of the race. I really didn't want to switch to my trail shoes which have zero cushioning. I feel like that was a good call especially since I don't usually change shoes in a race.

8th lap

It was really dark out. I have grown fond of using the green light on a headlamp instead of a red light or the normal beam. It doesn't bounce as much when running and gives you enough light to see the ground in front of you. Plus, it saves on battery life. I was still going strong and alternating between running and walking now. I wasn't tired but I was trying to save my legs as much as possible. During this lap, I grabbed the trekking poles. I wasn't sure if you were allowed to use them for this race because I didn't read the rules. I figured if they said something, I would only use them just for that lap. Luckily, they didn't say anything. Did I need to use them? No, but I feel it definitely helps save your legs and increases your walking speed if used correctly. I was going at a decent pace. I was walking more than running now. My pace was still good, around a 15–16 minute mile.

9th lap

I don't really remember much from this lap. Things were going ok, and I didn't have any breakdowns.

10th lap

I had a running buddy for a little bit. Alexis wanted to run with me for the lap but we decided that she would run to the halfway point with me. We went a little slower than I wanted, but I had company. That helped me during the second half of the lap. I think this is the first time she ran a non-obstacle race in the dark and it was pretty funny. Normally there are other people around but it was just the two of us until the aid station. She had her headphones in so it was a little difficult to talk to her. Mine were charging with Amy and hopefully they would last more than an hour.

11th lap

Amy was going to finish her last lap with me. I needed someone to run with me again. I was fine for the first few miles but then the cold got to me. I could barely hold the trekking poles. I was starting to sleepwalk. I was drained. I had Amy grab the poles so I could put my hands into my sweater. I wasn't eating or drinking enough and I knew it. My body was starting to revolt. Just close your eyes and take a break. It's alright if you don't finish, you weren't feeling good to start the race. You still did a 100k and that's good enough. I had to get out of my head. I just had to get to the truck, take another caffeine pill, get food, warm up, and get back out. Regroup, it'll be daylight soon. I put socks over my hands and headed back out after eating a sandwich.

12th lap

I was definitely slowing down. I think I was averaging a 16–17 minute mile. My math was a little off on what I had to do to finish by 3pm. Was there really a hard cutoff at 3pm or was I going to get a little leeway, I texted Amy to check how much of a chance I had at finishing on time. She met me at the halfway point and said I had extra time. I kind of felt before I met her, that I would be running these next laps for nothing. I would have to average a 2 hour, 15 minute lap pace to finish with wiggle room. Anything slower than that and I would be taking a big risk. No more long stops, I lollygagged too much earlier and it was coming to haunt me now.

How bad do you want this? Are you just going to quit now? Don't you want to do bigger races? Suck it up and start running. I remember what James messaged me earlier when I said I was behind schedule, "run faster." I shook my hand to the sky and cursed at James. He had texted me during the race to motivate me. Did I have enough in me to rail this out? Just keep moving forward, I could see Jen ahead of me. We had been going back and forth leading. My walking pace was just slightly slower than her running pace. Keep her in eyesight and just keep moving forward. Run a little bit here and there. The sun was starting to warm up the course again.

13th lap

I didn't stop for long. I grabbed a sandwich, refilled, and went back out. I took off my sweater and had my glasses and hat back on. I just had to keep going at a decent pace. I started to run a little more on this lap.

Last lap

I had about 2 hours and 25 minutes to finish this lap before the 3pm cutoff. I still wasn't 100% sure if I was going to get extra time and I didn't ask. How bad do you want it? If you want it, then finish before 3pm. During the race, I knew they were doing the *Bad water* lottery. I had to check to see if I got in. Nope, this was not my year and it added to my fuel to finish this race. No excuses. You are better than that. You can still run, so run. I pushed hard on this lap and I could definitely feel it. Something happened to the big toe on my right foot, I didn't have time to check, just finish.

Amy and the kids met me at the half way point, I don't remember stopping. I waved and kept running. This was it, the last 3.5 miles. I was making good time and gave myself a little buffer. Then I got to the sugar canes, should I cut that little section off? That would save me at least a quarter mile, if not more. I really debated it for a few minutes but decided against. I'd rather DNF than cut the course intentionally. Just run faster. I was trying to do the math in my head, how much farther versus the time left. Would I have to do a decent pace to finish on time? I made it to the last mile stretch. I had about 25 minutes left.

Just keep running, nothing fast, just don't walk.

I made it to the road. A guy pulled up to me to tell me I was the last runner on course and I should finish on time at this pace. I waved. I'm not sure if I said anything, I finished with about 10 minutes leftover. Where was everyone? Amy and the kids weren't there. I got my buckle and talked with the race director for a few minutes. I went and sat down. That's when Amy showed up.

With all of the races I've done, you would think I should be some kind of expert, not at all. Every race is a new learning experience and I keep making new mistakes. I have never had the perfect race where everything works out. Things come up and you have to overcome them. There were races where just enough went right to make up for my poor choices. The days that [that] doesn't happen might end up with a DNF, but I will still learn and get better. Over the years I've learned when to push and when to call it a day.

Will I still sign up for insane races with little training? Absolutely. I love terrible ideas. There's nothing better than finishing something you never thought you could. There's nothing special about me. Most people could accomplish similar with some training. Mental grit goes a long way. Most of my training was done when I didn't want to train. I was tired, hungry, cold, and hot—fill in the blank with any excuse.

Injuries sidelined me. People would say I was doing too much too soon. They could have been right but I wouldn't have accomplished what I did by following a normal training plan. Not many people would attempt half of the stuff I did, let alone in my timeline. My only advice would be to not train for an ultra marathon in two weeks. Listen to your body. Have fun pushing your limits. This is supposed to be fun.

I will keep pushing my limits and hopefully, this book inspires people to push their boundaries a little bit further. The people I have met may not realize how much they have helped me improve. I've definitely made mistakes along the way.

The story doesn't end here. There are a few races I left out. I'm still aiming big and pushing my limits even though I may end up with a few more DNFs than I want. Each one has been a learning experience, though at the time it definitely hurts. I hope you get a feeling of inspiration out of this book. Do some research and real training before an ultra marathon. Two weeks to train before the *GORUCK* World championship was not my best idea but I made an amazing friend and had a great time.

Injuries happen, but it's what you do after that makes you better. I'm very grateful that I'm still able to do what I can. I try not to take it as seriously as I did when I started. This is supposed to be fun. I will be out there cheering on anyone that shows up to a race. I may not know your backstop but I know you are out there trying your best. Hopefully, I see you out at my next race. Until then, keep pushing your limits.

8

Conclusion

With all of the races I've done, you would think I should be some kind of expert, not at all. Every race is a new learning experience and I keep making new mistakes. I have never had the perfect race where everything works out. Things come up and you have to overcome them. There were races where just enough went right to make up for my poor choices. The days that [that] doesn't happen might end up with a DNF, but I will still learn and get better. Over the years I've learned when to push and when to call it a day.

Will I still sign up for insane races with little training? Absolutely. I love terrible ideas. There's nothing better than finishing something you never thought you could. There's nothing special about me. Most people could accomplish similar with some training. Mental grit goes a long way. Most of my training was done when I didn't want to train. I was tired, hungry, cold, and hot—fill in the blank with any excuse.

Injuries sidelined me. People would say I was doing too much too soon. They could have been right but I wouldn't have accomplished what I did by following a normal training plan. Not many people would attempt half of the stuff I did, let alone in my timeline. My only advice would be to not train for an ultra marathon in two weeks. Listen to your body. Have fun pushing your limits. This is supposed to be fun.

I will keep pushing my limits and hopefully, this book inspires people to push their boundaries a little bit further. The people I have met may not realize how much they have helped me improve. I've definitely made mistakes along the way.

The story doesn't end here. There are a few races I left out. I'm still aiming big and pushing my limits even though I may end up with a few more DNFs than I want. Each one has been a learning experience, though at the time it definitely hurts. I hope you get a feeling of inspiration out of this book. Do some research and real training before an ultra marathon. Two weeks to train before the *GORUCK* World championship was not my best idea but I made an amazing friend and had a great time.

Injuries happen, but it's what you do after that makes you better. I'm very grateful that I'm still able to do what I can. I try not to take it as seriously as I did when I started. This is supposed to be fun. I will be out there cheering on anyone that shows up to a race. I may not know your backstop but I know you are out there trying your best. Hopefully, I see you out at my next race. Until then, keep pushing your limits.

List of races I've done so far

<u>2015</u>

Aug 15th Erie County 5k
Sept 19th Connor's 5k

<u>2016</u>

Sept 10th Beast on the Bay
Sept 17th Connor's 5k
Oct 8th Spartan Sprint Pittsburgh
Oct 29th EVL Half

<u>2017</u>

March 4th Greek Peak Sprint / Hurricane Heat
April 8th Charlotte Sprint
April 29th NJ Beast
May 6th Allegany Adventure run
May 21st Ohio Beast / Ohio Sprint
May 23rd Dirt Devil
May 31st Dirt Devil #2
June 3rd Virginia Super /Sprint
June 10th Chicago Super / HH12H
June 18th Black Swamp Dash
June 30th Athletes Unleashed WOD run
July 8th Palmerton Super / Sprint / HH
July 15th Chicago Rock N Roll Half and 5k
July 22nd Edinburgh Ultra Beast
August 8th Boston Super
August 12th Erie County Fair 5k
August 19th Moonlight Mud Run Black Swamp Dash
Sept 16th Killington Ultra (DNF)
Oct 2nd Rally at 3 Valley
Oct 7th Night of the Dead run

Oct 13th OCR Worlds
Oct 14th Volunteering at Pittsburgh Sprint
Oct 28th EVL Half
Nov 3rd HH12H NJ

2018

Feb 3rd Shale Hill
Feb 17th Beast of Burden 50 miler
April DNF at the NJ ultra
May 5th Viking Run
May 19th Bonefrog Endurance
May 27th Buffalo Marathon (PACER)
June 2nd Volunteering at Ohio Beast
June 3rd Girls on the Run(with Alexis)
June 16th Black Swamp Dash
July 11th Death Race (DNF)
July 28th Bonefrog Buffalo
August 4th Pacing the 50 miler Beast of Burden
August 10th Nor-AM
Sept 3rd GORUCK light Pittsburgh
Sept 8th Bonefrog Boston
Sept 15th Killington Ultra
Sept 28th GORUCK Tough MOG Mile
Sept 29th Light
Sept 30th Rally at 3 Valley (Barefoot)
Oct 6th Night of the Dead
Oct 13th Pittsburgh Volunteered Sprint(Ran Super)
Oct 20th Bonefrog DC Endurance
Oct 26th weekend THE QUADFECTA
Nov 10th Bonefrog

2019

Feb 16th Beast of Burden 100

March 2nd Buffalo Shamrock volunteering

March 9th Fight for Air Climb (30lb ruck)

March 17th GORUCK Tough/ light Pittsburgh

April 9th GORUCK light Cleveland

April 12th Columbus Star Course 50 miler

April 28th Rochester Half (Pacing with 20lb ruck)

May 9th Team Assessment (DNF)

May 18th Bonefrog New England

May 25th Buffalo HTL

June 1st TOUR DE CURE with Joe D

June 8th Bonefrog NJ (Trident with Joe D)

June 15th Black Swamp Dash

June 22nd Indian mud run

July 9th Death Race

Aug 23rd Cincinnati Star course 50 miler(Nick and Rob)

Sept 7th Savage race (volunteer and race)

Sept 20th GORUCK Constellation

Sept 21st Rochester Marathon (PACER)

Oct 12th Stadium Blitz

Oct 19th Pittsburgh Stadium Spartan

Oct 27th Chestnut ridge 10k

2020

March 7th Trail Methods last runner standing

July 1st STTC summer tri #2

Oct 24th EVL half

Sept 5th Cassadagaman 70.3

2021

Feb 6th Frozen 50k
April 24th Hyner 50k
May 8th Happy Half
March 27th Georgia Death Race (DNF)
April 30th SISU endurance
May 30th Cassadaga running festival
May 15th Keys 100
June 19th Leadville 26.2
July 31st Mighty Mosquito 100
Eastern States 100
Sept 4th Cassadagaman 70.3
Nov 25th Turkey trot
Oct 23rd EVL half
Nov 19th GORUCK World Championship 50 miler

2022

Jan 15th Operation OCALA
Jan 29th Skydive 100
March 27th Bonefrog Virginia Beach
May 28th Buffalo Marathon
June 18th Black Swamp Dash
March 19th Pistol Ultra 100
May 7th Fight for Air Climb
May 21st Keys 100 (DNF)
April 1st Vernal Equinox 48 hour ruck
June 18th Black Swamp Dash
June 25th Indian Mud Run (DNF)
July 16th Operation Dragon's Dance
Aug 6th Mighty Mosquito 100 (DNF)
Aug 13th Eastern States 100 (DNF)
Aug 20th KIA memorial march 10k

Bonefrog Buffalo 2018

Beast on the Bay 2016

Goruck Star Course Columbus 2019

Killington Ultra 2018

Texas Roadhouse 5k

Beast of Burden Summer

GORUCK Championship

Keys 100 - Florida Keys

Skydive Ultra 100

Death Race, 2021

Kimball and I after SISU

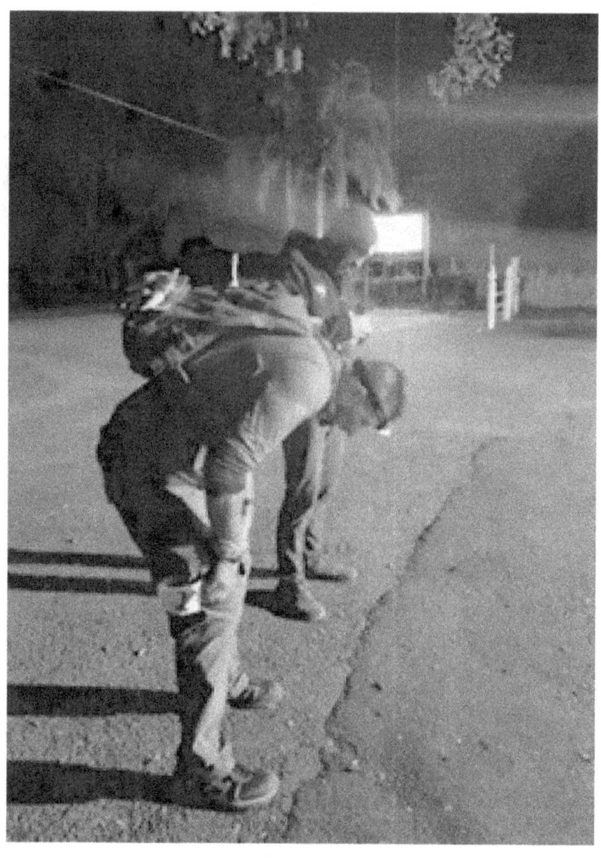

Operation OCALA 2021

The Viking Challenge - At Sunny Hill